SOLDIERS' SONGS AND SLANG
OF THE GREAT WAR

OSPREY
PUBLISHING

SOLDIERS' SONGS
AND SLANG OF
THE GREAT WAR

Martin Pegler

First published in Great Britain in 2014 by Osprey Publishing,
PO Box 883, Oxford, OX1 9PL, UK
PO Box 3985, New York, NY 10185-3985, USA
E-mail: info@ospreypublishing.com

Osprey Publishing is part of the Osprey Group

A CIP catalogue record for this book is available from the British Library

Martin Pegler has asserted his right under the Copyright, Designs and Patents Act,
1988, to be identified as the Author of this Work.

ISBN: 978 1 4728 0415 0
E-pub ISBN: 978 1 4728 0929 2
PDF ISBN: 978 1 4728 0928 5

Typeset in Century Schoolbook, Bodoni & Verve
Originated by PDQ Digital Media Solutions, Suffolk
Printed in China through Worldprint Ltd.

14 15 16 17 18 19   10 9 8 7 6 5 4 3 2 1

Osprey Publishing is supporting the Woodland Trust, the UK's leading woodland
conservation charity, by funding the dedication of trees.

www.ospreypublishing.com

Front cover: Illustration taken from a recruitment poster of the Great War. (Mary Evans Picture
Library)

To all of the Great War veterans we knew, whose

courage, humour and modesty made them

unique. It was a privilege to have known you all.

ACKNOWLEDGEMENTS

Thank you to Lyn Macdonald, who introduced me to so many veterans of the Great War way back in the 1970s, and to Richard Dunning, who for the last 40 years had made it a personal crusade to prevent the Great War from becoming just another forgotten conflict. Thanks too, for help with images, to Clive Gilbert, Barry Lees and Peter Smith. Special thanks also to Kate Moore at Osprey who deemed this a worthy project, and Emily Holmes, who had to edit it! Last, but not least, to my long-suffering wife Katie, who has accepted with her usual tolerance my absences whilst I hid in my study, attempting to be creative.

CONTENTS

INTRODUCTION

In a single volume there are limits as to how much can be covered in such a vast field as the songs, slang and terminology of the First World War. One could write (and indeed authors have written) books covering just one of the areas that this book encompasses. The first attempt to put all of this into a single volume was made by John Brophy and Eric Partridge in 1931 under the title *Songs and Slang of the British Soldier*. It was of necessity incomplete, leaving out much of the slang and verses of songs that were considered too crude for the rather more delicate sensibilities of the readers of that time. Although enlarged and updated in 1965 it remained heavily edited. It was, however, the first book on the Great War that I ever purchased and it was responsible for awakening my own interest, enabling me to be able to sing all of the songs from memory by the age of 12. I'm sure my parents wished that they had a normal son who just liked the Beatles.

The 50th anniversary of the end of the war in 1968 did much to raise awareness of the subject and the subsequent release of the remarkable film *Oh What A Lovely War* in 1969 reached new audiences who would not normally have regarded the First World War as anything other than a distant historic event. My wife and I were very fortunate in the late 1970s and early 1980s to visit and interview dozens of veterans; their conversation was often peppered with the language of the trenches and it took little persuasion to start them singing long-forgotten songs. I made as many notes as I could, and these have miraculously survived assorted house moves and a disastrous fire.

It seemed to me, with the approach of the centenary of the war in 2014, that it was time for a properly updated and enlarged version of Brophy and Partidge's work, so I have incorporated as much as possible of their material into this book. Of course, due to space constraints I have had to be selective in some areas but the text covers the most commonly found words, expressions and songs of the period, including those words considered, not so many years ago, to be obscene.

A surprising number of songs will still be familiar to us, such as 'If You Were The Only Girl In The World' and 'I'm Always Chasing Rainbows' but it is probably the slang that will cause the most surprise, as so much of our language today still uses words and phrases that first saw the light of day in the trenches of France and Flanders. As common examples, people often refer to their loose change as 'shrapnel' and of course everyone 'chats' to friends, but few understand that the widespread dissemination of these words was a result of the war.

Gradually these and many other words and phrases have been absorbed into modern English, without anyone really noticing. Still more expressions, such as 'over the top', have been recently reinvented, albeit with a slightly altered meaning.

I sincerely hope that this book will enlighten, amuse and occasionally surprise the reader. If I have missed out any vital entries (and I'm sure I must have) I apologise and any errors contained are, of course, entirely mine. I hope you'll find the subject as fascinating as I have done.

Martin Pegler
Combles, France.

PART 1

SOLDIERS' SLANG

The English language reflects our old and very mixed culture, and like most languages it is not static. It continues to change with time, many words falling out of use, whilst others are adopted and sometimes adapted. As an example of how much it has changed, try reading a text in 14th-century English. It is all but incomprehensible to anyone but a specialized historian. Even much of the English of Shakespeare's time is now bewildering to our modern eyes, as those who recall having to study it at school will know. Latin, Norse, Germanic and French words have all contributed to what we know and speak today. Whilst every generation thinks of its language as contemporary, much of the English spoken by the men of the Great War generation was that of the previous two or three centuries. In addition, at the turn of the 20th century, there were huge linguistic differences to be found within the regions of the British Isles, possibly more so than there are today, for there was no standardized BBC English. Regional accents and words were quite unintelligible to men from different areas. At the turn of the 20th century this mattered very little, as few men travelled outside of their native areas to work or live, but that was to change dramatically post-1914.

The British Expeditionary Force (BEF) that arrived in France in 1914 was, in military terms, a tough, experienced and well-trained force which also had its own language, a polyglot mix of words and phrases collected from decades of service around the empire, particularly in India and the Middle East. The BEF suffered terribly in the early months of the war and huge numbers of reinforcements were required. These came in the form of reserve territorials and large numbers of volunteers drawn from every county and every level of British society. Irish, Scots and Welsh mixed with Geordies, East and West countrymen and Cockneys. The men who comprised the bulk of these soldiers and sailors came from civilian backgrounds where life was unimaginably hard and society provided no support in bad times. It is a shocking statistic that one third of all the men who volunteered for service during the war were suffering to a greater or lesser extent from the effects of malnutrition. For many of those men, tough as it was, army life was an improvement on what they had left behind. They had their own regional language but as most were trained by regular army non-commissioned officers they absorbed much additional slang.

However, as a result of the unexpected introduction of trench warfare in late 1914, there arose a *lingua franca* that reflected not only the unique, self-deprecating humour of the British, but also their stoicism. Without doubt, a certain amount had an historic precedent, the best example being the unique form of street argot that evolved in the East End of London, known as rhyming slang. Although still debated this is thought to have begun as a means of private communication between costermongers and street sellers sometime in the early 19th century. However, a great many of the words and phrases were simply made up by the soldiers in response to the conditions in which they found themselves.

There was also another element to the language of the Great War which prior to 1914 had barely existed and this arose as a result of the large numbers of educated middle-class men who had enlisted. These men had had little exposure to traditional earthy, bawdy working class language, and when in the ranks they found it difficult to accept. Charles Carrington wrote that the hardest thing to bear was '… the constant use of the "F" word'* by his fellow soldiers. Contemporary autobiographies of the immediate post-war period virtually ignored the use of swear words, but swearing was endemic in the army and navy. However, these new soldiers from the middle and upper-middle class, who under normal circumstances would never have joined the army except perhaps as officers, brought with them their own ways of communicating and they exerted an influence on how the soldiers spoke and also the types of songs they sang.

---

* C.E. Carrington, *Soldier From the Wars Returning,* Hutchinson, London, 1965, p.67.

MILITARY SLANG, TERMINOLOGY AND POPULAR PHRASES

AAA	Ack, Ack, Ack. 'Stop' on a Morse buzzer. Used in all signal messages. See also *phonetic alphabet* and Appendix 1.
A, B, C, D	The four companies of an infantry battalion. See Appendix 2.
Abdul	A Turkish soldier. See also *Jacko, Johnny*.
Abort	The German word for a toilet or latrine, brought back by prisoners of war. It later became used to signify the abandoning of a plan or mission.
About Turn	The village of Hebertune, from where the 56th London Division

attacked Gommecourt on 1 July 1916.

abris
A French word for a *shelter* or *dug-out*. Mostly used by British officers.

accessory
The code word for poison gas.

according to plan
An oft used expression in the press, signifying that something had worked without any undue problems. Later in the war it was used by troops in a more cynical manner.

ace
Although the definition of an ace varied from country to country, it was generally accepted that a combat pilot who shot down five or more enemy aircraft achieved ace status.

ack-ack
Anti-aircraft gun or fire, from the AA of the phonetic alphabet. See also *Archie*.

Adam and Eve
Believe.

addressed to
Aimed at, usually of a shell or bullet.

adjutant
Usually the aide to the commanding officer with the rank of captain. Responsible for much of the daily running of a battalion.

adjutant's nightmare
The army code book, which was extremely complex.

Adrian hut
The French equivalent of the ubiquitous British *Nissen hut*.

adrift
A naval expression from the mid-19th century meaning absent without leave. See also *AWOL*.

ADS	An advanced dressing station, close to the line, where the more seriously wounded could be attended to.
aerial dart	Also known as *aerodart* or *flechette*, this was a machine-turned steel dart dropped on troops by aviators in the early years of the war. Dropped from 100ft a dart was capable of traversing the body of a man from head to toe. Deadly but wildly inaccurate, it was largely abandoned by 1915.
aerial torpedo	Specifically the large naval torpedo dropped by aircraft, but later adopted by infantrymen to cover any form of large *trench mortar* shell.
aerodart	See *aerial dart*.
AFC	Air Force Cross. See Appendix 6.
AFM	Air Force Medal. See Appendix 6.
afters	A second course, often meaning a dessert or pudding.
agony, an	A newly joined regimental subaltern.
aggravation	Railway station.
aid post	The forward-most position found in the front lines from where Royal Army Medical Corps (RAMC) staff could attend to wounded men. Sometimes called the regimental aid post.
aide-de-camp (ADC)	a staff officer attached to act as assistant to a general.

ak-dum

A regular army expression from the Hindi meaning 'at once' but later transposed as the German 'Achtung' or 'look out'.

Albatross

A German single-seater fighter aircraft, introduced in December 1916.

Albert

The town in Picardy closest to the Somme front lines. It became famous for the statue on top of the tower of the basilica, known as the *Leaning Virgin*, chained in place after being hit by a shell in 1915. She was a landmark for miles around and all who served on the Somme would have seen her. See also *Fanny Durack*.

all cut

A military expression from the mid-20th century meaning upset or bothered.

alley

Run away, from the French 'allez'.

alleyman

A German, from the French 'Allemand'.

Ally Slopers Cavalry

Army Service Corps (ASC). Alexander 'Ally' Sloper was a comic strip character portrayed as a lazy, scheming ne'er-do-well who disliked any form of work. It was applied to the ASC because of their relatively safe jobs, good rations and high pay. They were also referred to as the 'Army Safety Corps' or 'the Ascots'.

ammo Ammunition, usually for small arms. Britain manufactured over 14 billion rounds of .303in ammunition during the war. See also *SAA*.

ammonal An explosive made from ammonium nitrate and aluminium powder. Although it required a powerful detonator and was hygroscopic, or water-absorbing, it was far cheaper than TNT and was widely used in *Mills grenades* and for mining.

ammo's The army boot, properly known as the 'ammunition boot'.

Angels of Mons Mythical angels who were said to have helped the British Army during the battle of Mons, invented by Welsh author Arthur Machen. Despite his insistence that they were purely imaginary, many popular papers and magazines ran the story as fact.

anti-frostbite A lard-like substance supplied to troops to combat frostbite and *trench foot*. Later *whale oil* was substituted, but it smelled foul and soldiers hated it.

Any more for any more? The orderly's popular shout offering seconds of something – tea, bread, bully stew. Sometimes used by men running *Crown and Anchor* games.

Anzac Australian and New Zealand Army Corps. Named after the abbreviated form of the Corps HQ at Gallipoli. Popularly used in the press, it was seldom used by soldiers, who never referred to themselves as Anzacs, but preferred the more familiar *Aussie* or *Kiwi*.

APM
Assistant provost marshal. The *Military Police* equivalent of a chief constable. See also *Red Caps*.

apples and pears
Stairs.

après la guerre
One of dozens of French phrases adopted into common usage. It had two meanings, the first as a cynical observation 'when will the general visit the trenches?' 'Oh, après la guerre.' The second was a more thoughtful sentiment referring to better times when the war had finished. It was popularized in a music-hall song (reproduced later in this book) of 1917–18.

Archie
From 'Archibald', anti-aircraft fire. Introduced by pilots who had flown pre-war. The origin is debatable, some sources citing Archibald sewage farm near Brooklands in Surrey, which created notorious air turbulence, the same effect as the exploding shells. Other sources cite the music-hall song by George Robey 'Archibald! Certainly Not', which is reproduced later in this book.

area commandant　　A senior officer responsible for providing billets and recreational facilities in towns or rest areas behind the lines. See also *town major*.

area shoot　　An artillery term for the bombardment of a specified area to destroy enemy trenches, roads or troop concentrations.

argue the toss　　To dispute long and loudly.

armour-piercing bullets　　Adopted by the Germans in 1915, they were originally for use in aircraft, but were supplied in small numbers to snipers to penetrate steel British *loophole plates*. They became more widely available as the war progressed.

Armstrong hut　　A practical, small wood and canvas hut.

army　　The British Army was made up of five armies, sub-divided into army corps. See Appendix 2 for a breakdown of units.

Army Form SH - One - T　　Pointless army paperwork. See also *Bumf*.

Arrival　　The sound of an incoming shell. Experienced soldiers could tell the type and direction almost instantly.

arse　　The bottom. It dates from the mid-17th century and was even then considered vulgar. During the war, it was a generic term with literally dozens of uses and meanings, eg: to kick someone's arse: to hurry them up; arse-off: to be late; arsing about: to fool around; arse crawler: a sycophant.

arsty Slow down, from a Hindi word.

artillery duel When the guns of both sides were employed virtually non-stop. The infantry were usually the recipients of the shells, although occasionally an artillery unit would concentrate its fire on a known enemy artillery position.

as you were The military equivalent of acknowledging and ignoring a command given in error.

Asiatic Annie A large-calibre Turkish gun at Gallipoli.

Asquiths French matches that often failed to light. From Prime Minister Asquith's famous 'Wait and see' speech in response to the serious pre-war unrest in Britain.

assault course Originally the bayonet-fighting course in training camps. Later it became any arduous physical course.

Aussie An Australian soldier, derived from the word Australia.

avec Borrowed from the French and used when ordering a coffee with added spirit, usually rum or brandy as in 'I want a café avec.'

AWOL Absent without leave.

Ayrton fan Also known as *flapper*, a gas-dispersing fan invented by Mrs Hertha Ayrton in 1915. Over 100,000 were manufactured.

babbling brook or babbler An army cook.

Baby A small Sopwith biplane used by the Royal Naval Air Service (RNAS) at the beginning of the war.

Backs to the wall A reference to the famous order by General Haig issued on 11 April 1918 in response to the massive German attack originally launched in March 1918. Had the Germans broken through Allied lines it could have forced the Allies to concede an armistice with unfavourable terms.

bags A lot of, as in 'Got any rum? Yes, bags of it.' Also an abbreviated term for sandbags. See also *over the bags or over the top*.

Balaclava cap A practical knitted tube that could be worn as a hat underneath the steel helmet in winter, or wrapped round the neck as a scarf. Supposedly invented just after the Crimean War similar types have been depicted in paintings as far back as the 15th century. See also *cap comforter*.

ball and bat Hat.

ball of lead Head.

The Communication Trench Problem – Whether to walk along the top and risk it, or do another mile of this. (Bruce Bairnsfather, author's collection)

balloon

Used in the context of 'What time does the balloon go up?' In other words, 'When does an event begin?' Also relating to the many observation balloons strung across the front lines.

balloonatics

Those working in or with the observation balloons.

band, to follow the

Literally following one's regimental band. Later to mean keeping to a set method or procedure.

Bandagehem, Dosinghem, Mendinghem

Aid posts in Flanders, inevitably corrupted to 'Bandaging 'em, Dosing 'em and Mending 'em'.

bandolier or bandoleer

From the wooden tubes of the 17th century used to carry gunpowder. In the First World War, this had been modified into either the Pattern 1903 leather or Pattern 1908 webbing equipment with separate ammunition pouches. The leather bandolier did survive however for use with mounted troops and engineers.

bandook or bundook

The Hindi word for a musket or rifle, taken from the original word meaning a cross-bow. Brought to the Western Front by regular army troops and widely adopted. See also *hipe*.

Bangalore torpedo

Invented in 1912 by Captain McClintock of the British Indian Army whilst based at Bangalore, it comprised threaded sections of 5ft-long steel pipe, with a diameter of about 8in, so any desired length could be made up. Packed with explosive, it would clear a 5ft-wide path through wire entanglements and was first introduced on the Western Front in 1915. Similar devices are still in use today.

Banjo

Australian for a shovel.

bantams

Battalions formed from short men, typically under 5ft 4in.

bapoo or barpoo

Mad, crazy, from a Hindi word. Adopted by pilots to describe a crash. 'Jimmy went bapoo yesterday.' See also *batchy*.

barbed wire

The vast protective entanglements strung on wooden or metal stakes (see *screw picket*) across the whole front line. They were waist high and could be dozens of feet wide and uncut wire was a serious impediment to any attacking force. 'On the wire' became an expression for any plan that failed or for men that had disappeared.

barker

A sausage (from a popular song about a dog). Sometimes used by officers when referring to their revolver.

barrack room lawyer   A know-it-all, or argumentative soldier.

barrage   Originally the term for the protective fire laid in front of or behind troops to provide protection. A *creeping barrage* was one that moved forwards as the infantry advanced. A *box barrage* surrounded a very specific area, often used during *trench raids*. 'Lifting a barrage' was the technique of increasing range to move the barrage forward. See also *bracketing, registering*.

base, the   That dreamed-of place where there were comfy beds, good food and no fatigues. Few infantrymen ever sampled it.

base hospital   Huge hospitals, usually near railways or canals to facilitate moving casualties. Wounded requiring long-term treatment were evacuated to England; less serious cases stayed until deemed fit. By 1918 there were 83 such hospitals.

base wallah   A soldier employed at a base area, so living a safe and comfortable life. Often instructors who had never visited the front line. See also *bull ring*.

bat and wicket   Ticket.

batchy A common term for mad, but also meaning a bit daft or losing one's nerve. From a Hindi word.

bathmats Derogatory word for trench *duckboards*.

batman An officer's servant. From the early 19th-century term referring to the soldier responsible for looking after the officer's bat or *pack–horse*. Although the term 'bat' has long since fallen into disuse, *batman* survived. See also *bloke*.

battalion The largest of the front-line combat formations; during the war the strength of a line battalion could be as low as 500 men due to losses, leave etc. See Appendix 2.

batter, to go on the Originally from the 1830s referring to prostitutes plying their wares on the streets. As with many expressions the meaning shifted with time and by 1914 it meant to go on a drinking binge or indulge in riotous behaviour.

battery A unit of artillery under command of a colonel. Depending on the size of the guns, a battery might comprise anything from three or four guns up to a dozen.

battle assembly or battle position The departure point for an attack.

battle bowler Officers' slang for the steel helmet.

See also *tin hat*. Also known as *lid*, *pot*, *pudding basin*, *steel jug*.

battle order
Also known as *fighting order*. The reduced equipment carried by a soldier into combat. Typically the large pack and greatcoat were left behind but this was more than made up for by additional items such as spade, pick, grenades, extra ammunition etc. Many soldiers actually found themselves carrying 60–70lb in additional weight when attacking.

battle police
The armed *Military Police* on duty behind the lines during an attack. Their job was to ensure that stragglers or the reluctant were sent forward. Only wounded men were exempt. MPs were seldom seen in the front lines and were the object of great contempt among fighting troops. See also *Red Caps*.

battle surplus
Troops allocated as reinforcements, sometimes called 'first reinforcements' or 'cadre'.

bay
See *fire bay*, *traverse*, *trench*.

be good
One of several general expressions when parting, mostly used facetiously. In full it was 'Be good, and if you can't be good, be careful' which had vague sexual overtones. See also *cheer-o*, *chin-chin*, *toodle-pip*.

Beachy Bill

Similar to Asiatic Annie, a large-calibre Turkish artillery piece used at Gallipoli.

beat

Also *dead beat* and 'beat(en) to the wide'. Exhausted, worn out. The author recalls his grandfather (a Great War veteran) regularly using the last of these terms. See also *whacked*.

beat(en) to a frazzle

Totally beaten or worn out. From the American South, mid-18th-century term meaning to be whipped with the frayed end of a rope. See also *dead beat*.

beef hearts

Beans supplied in tins, from the rhyming slang for 'farts'.

BEF

The British Expeditionary Force, the pre-war regular army sent into France in August 1914 which comprised almost 248,000 regular and territorial soldiers. By the end of the fighting in 1914, the bulk of this army had been killed, wounded or captured, although they did stem the German advance. See also *Old Contemptibles*.

Before you come up

A popular put-down often used by NCOs on private soldiers. In essence it meant 'I know more than you do, am tougher than you, have experienced more than you ever will and am generally a better soldier than you will ever be.'

beer and skittles, life's not all
Unpleasant or difficult, dating from the 1860s, it was a predominantly southern-English expression.

bees and honey
Money. Sometimes shortened to just 'bees'.

beetle-crushers
The army boots. These were hobnailed and did not have the highly polished toe cap beloved by modern drill sergeants. They were hard to break in but comfortable and durable, though not waterproof. See also *ammo's*.

bell tent
Named because of its shape, it was supported by a central pole and guy ropes. It was said that it was perfectly designed to hold 16 men in equal discomfort.

berm
In its medieval context, a berm was the space between a defensive *parapet* and a steep-walled ditch, intended to reduce pressure, and thus the likelihood of collapse. By 1914 it had come to mean a ledge in a trench or on a *parapet* on which grenades, ammunition or flares were stored.

Bert
A shortened form of the Somme town of Albert.

Bertha
A German nickname for any large gun. See also *Big Bertha*, *Emma*.

bevvy
A drink, probably from the mid-19th-century French 'biberon', a baby's

bottle. The term was used at Eton and Winchester colleges as 'bevers' in the late 19th century to denote afternoon tea.

Big Bertha
(Grosse Bertha) Specifically a Krupp-built super-heavy 42cm howitzer firing an 1,900lb shell. Latterly it became a generic term for any large-calibre enemy guns, in particular the *Paris Gun*. The *Bouncing Bertha* was another huge 42cm German artillery gun. This was a piece of drollery on the part of the soldiers, for the last thing these colossal shells would do was bounce.

Big Boys
Big artillery shells or guns.

big noise
An Americanism dating from pre-1910 denoting a senior officer, politician or anyone with considerable authority.

Big Willie
The Kaiser, Wilhelm II. See also *Little Willie*.

Bill Adams or BA
A euphemism for bugger all. See also *FA*.

Bill Harris
Bilharzia, a common river-borne disease found in Egypt, Salonika and Mesopotamia.

Billet
Originating in the 1880s as a prison term denoting a soft or easy job, by the First World War it meant anywhere where troops could be housed. These ranged from barns, tents, occupied or empty houses to

(rarely for the private soldier) even chateaux. The term was widely used during the war in many different contexts, thus 'a cushy billet' was a comfy resting place, whereas a random bullet hitting a man could be described as 'having found a billet'.

Billy Wells   A heavy shell named after the English boxer Bombardier Wells. See also *Johnson or Jack Johnson*.

binge   *c.* 1880. In its original form it came from Oxford University and was a student term meaning to go out with friends to cheer oneself up. Getting drunk was frequent but not inevitable; singing and eating also played a big part. It was predominantly an officers' term, but by 1918 had been widely adopted to mean getting drunk. See also *blind or blind drunk*.

bint   Arabic term for a daughter, used to refer to any young woman.

bird   Also a young woman, but a gentler term than 'bint' often identifying women as a sweetheart as in 'My bird and I will get wed when I'm back in Blighty.' It has Regency origins and was used originally in the context of prostitution.

bird cage   A defensive camp built in Salonika in 1915–16, but also referring to an emplacement occupied by snipers.

biscuits   Two definitions exist. The first were the small, square army mattresses, three to a bed, used in barracks. They were generally regarded as being as comfortable as the army issue food of the same name. The hard-tack biscuits issued were naval ships' biscuits made from flour, water and salt. As rations they were famous for their concrete-like consistency, but when crushed and mixed with water and raisins or anything else to hand they could be boiled or fried and were relatively palatable.

bitch, to   In its late 18th-century form, 'bitch' was the most offensive term one could use for a woman. Later it changed its meaning into 'to make a bitch about…' meaning to complain loudly and this was then abbreviated in use into 'to bitch'.

bivvy or bivouack   To stop for the night. Also a simple shelter using a couple, or more, of laced-together waterproof sheets supported by a central horizontal pole. Pleasant in summer, miserable in winter.

Black Hand Gang, the   A selected or volunteer party for a risky enterprise, such as trench

When One Would Like to Start an Offensive on One's Own
Recipe for Feeling Like This – Bully, biscuits, no coke, and leave just cancelled. (Bruce Bairnsfather, author's collection)

raiding. It appears to be a term originating in the trenches in 1915–16.

Black Maria Traditionally a black-painted prison van, it was one of many terms for a specific type of shell, in this case the large German howitzer shells that burst with a thick pall of black smoke. See also *coal box*, *Johnson or Jack Johnson*.

bladder of fat A hat, either soft or steel. See also *tit-for-tat*.

blanked Drunk, from the French 'vin blanc', white wine.

blanket drill The afternoon sleep beloved of soldiers serving in hot climates. Later used to define any form of sleep.

blasted or blarsted A euphemism for 'bloody' dating from the mid-17th century. Mostly used by men from the south of England. Also referring to a landscape that has been reduced to a wasteland by shellfire.

Blighty The derivation of this word is unclear, as it could have originated either from the Hindi word 'bilaik' meaning a foreign place or country, or from the Arabic 'beladi' meaning 'my own country'. However, to the soldiers it was a term that meant one thing only: home. It became a word of almost mystical power, for it signified a former existence in a different world. *Blighty* represented a fairyland, where life was comfortable, familiar and peaceful. It was populated by family and friends, a total antithesis to his existence in the front line. It also became used as an adjective, such as 'This is like real Blighty bread.'

Blighty bag　　The small cloth bag containing the personal kit of a wounded man. In theory it should follow him to his eventual destination, but it seldom did.

Blighty one, a　　A wound bad enough to cause a man to be sent home to recuperate. Very minor or mortal wounds were treated in France, but most men dreamed of getting the perfect *Blighty*, a light wound in a non-vital part of the body, such as shoulder or leg. Comrades would often shake the hands of men being carried out on stretchers, part in congratulations, part in envy.

blimp　　Originally naval slang for a small dirigible, towed behind destroyers with a lookout whose job was to spot for submarines. Later adopted by the Royal Air Force (RAF).

blind or blind drunk　　As a noun it had a similar meaning to *binge*, as an adjective it meant roaring drunk and as a verb it was to curse someone or something roundly. It dates back to the 17th century and would appear to refer to the lack of focused eyesight when very drunk. See also *binge*, *blanked*, *blotto*, *pissed*, *squiffy*, *tight*, *zig-zag*. It was also used to describe a *dud* shell.

blind ten, twenty, thirty Even 10, 20, 30 used in card games.

blinking A lesser version of bleeding or *bloody*.

blip or blipping Rotary aircraft engines had no throttle so ran at a constant speed. To slow them down a 'blip' switch cut the ignition to several cylinders. It had inherent dangers in that fuel was still being sucked into the cylinders and switching the ignition back on could result in an explosion.

blob A glass of beer, primarily a pre-war military term.

block, to do one's, or lose one's A complex expression with many meanings, but in the context of the Great War it was popular particularly with Australian troops, and meant to lose one's temper, or senses.

blockhouse A stand-alone fortified position, normally of reinforced concrete. Of medieval origin, used to describe a fortified position built to hold artillery. The majority of blockhouses on the Western Front were of German construction.

bloke
A mid-19th-century naval term originally meaning the commander of a warship. Suggestions for its origin are varied: Dutch 'blok', a fool or idiot; Hindi 'loke' I, a man; or even an Irish word 'gloak', meaning a chap or fellow. During the war its meaning was almost exclusively that of an officer's *batman* or servant.

blood money
Wound compensation, self-explanatory.

bloody
The most often-used swear word in the army as both adjective and verb. It can be traced back to the mid-17th century. Mostly it was used by soldiers as an epithet 'I've had it up to bloody here with the shelling' or an insertion 'Stew again, hoo-bloody-ray' or a direct curse 'that sergeant is a bloody bastard'. Also used as a euphemism 'blurry'.

blotto
Drunk. Perhaps derived from the properties of blotting paper in soaking up liquids. Curiously, the Oxford English Dictionary defined blotting paper as 'bibulous'. See also *binge, blanked, blind, pissed, squiffy, tight, zig-zag*.

41

blow a mine To detonate a mine. See *mine*.

blown to buggery Blown to pieces, of either a person or an object.

blue, in the A corruption of 'into the wild blue yonder' meaning something that has gone wrong, or is very wide of the mark. Originally a shooting term referring to a bullet or shell that has missed its target by a very wide margin. Mainly used by Australian troops.

blue cross shell A shell marked with a large blue cross filled with a mix of high explosive and Diphenylchloroarsine, which was not actually a gas but a fine powder that clogged respirators and also attacked the nose, throat and sinuses causing sneezing and irritation. It did not actually work very efficiently and by 1917 was largely superseded by other more lethal forms of gas. See also *green cross shell*, *yellow cross shell*.

Blue Devils The 'Diables Bleus', or French Chasseurs Alpins.

blue unction A blue-coloured ointment used in the treatment of pubic lice, or crabs.

blues Regulation hospital blue uniform. Wearing one's blues in public in England was usually a free pass to beer and other hospitality.

bob tack Army brass polish.

bobbajee   An army cook, from a Hindi word.

bobberry   Used in the Regular Army in India to describe a fracas, largely redundant by 1915.

Bobby (or Bobby's) job   An easy, or *cushy* job. Its origin is unknown. It is believed the post-war term 'Bob-a-Job' originated from it.

bob-down or bob-man   An anti-aircraft or, latterly, anti-gas sentry, whose warning caused men to disappear with as much haste as possible. Sometimes confused with 'bobber', an unpopular sort who acted as an informer to NCOs.

Boche or Bosche   The French slang term for a German believed to be from 'caboche', a slang word for cabbage and used as 'tête de boche' or blockhead. Its date of origin is unclear but it was in use during the Franco-Prussian War of 1870–71. In the early years of the Great War, the French re-introduced it as a generic term for Germans, as well as 'sales boches' or filthy Germans. After 1915 seldom used by other ranks but it continued to be used by officers. By 1918 it had been supplanted by other terms such as *Fritz, Hun, Jerry, Squarehead*.

body snatchers   See *stretcher bearers*.

bollocked   To be admonished or given a verbal dressing down for a misdemeanour.

bollocks   From *c*. 1910, the testicles.

Originally an old English word, 'ballocky or bollicky' when it was used to describe someone who was left-handed or clumsy. By 1914–18 it was much used by soldiers to describe something that was ineffective or bad.

bolo A late war word for a spy, taken from the name of Paul Bolo, also known as Bolo Pasha, a French financier who spied for the Germans. He was executed on 17 April 1918.

bomb proof A shelter that provided the barest of overhead protection from *shell splinters* or from *shrapnel*.

bomb the chat To brag or make implausible claims.

Bombardier Fritz A convoluted British corruption of 'pommes frites', or chips. Ordered with eggs it was a hugely popular dish when out of the line and most French houses would offer it to hungry troops.

bombers Grenade men, selected for their strong throwing arms.

bombing post A strong point in a trench manned by the *bombers*, designed to halt or slow down enemy infiltration. See also *bomb-stop*.

bomb-proof job One that kept a man in a safe environment.

bomb-stop A barricade or traverse in a trench,

usually manned by *bombers*. See also *bombing post*.

bon
From the French for 'good'. When used as an adjective, it signified something or some place that was acceptable. 'The rations are tres bon today.' But it could also simply be used to signify acceptance. 'You're on sentry tonight.' 'Bon.' Oddly, when used in a negative form, the French 'pas bon' was ignored, the Anglicized version being 'no bon'. See also *trey bon*.

bon (or bonne) chance
Good luck. From the French, and much used in the trenches.

bon for the bust
First used by French civilians offering food to the troops, its origin is unclear. However, it meant 'good to eat'.

bon sonte
Cheers, an English derivation of the French 'bonne santé' or good health.

bon time
Having a good time. 'We had a bon time in that estaminet last night.'

bonce
The head. In the mid-19th century a bonce was a London expression for a large marble, and it became a commonplace word among schoolboys.

bone
To borrow, usually without the owner's permission; from the late 17th century and probably taken from the concept of a dog making off with a bone.

boneyard

A cemetery. Also known as 'bone orchard'. Mostly a late 19th-century Canadian expression but sometimes used by British troops.

bonza or bonzer

An Australianism for good. Perhaps from the mining word 'bonanza'.

booze

First recorded in print in 1611, it meant a drunkard. However, by the early 20th century 'boozer' was a much used Australian and New Zealand word for a public house. By association going for a drink became 'boozing'.

bosom chums

Lice, the scourge of the trenches. See also *chatt*.

Bouncing Bertha

See *Big Bertha*.

Bow Street

The orderly room, from the old London term for the police court.

bowler, to be given the

Demobilization, from the issue of civilian clothing. Also to be 'given a bowler', which implied losing one's job. Normally used only of senior officers who were sent home.

box barrage

A three-sided artillery *barrage* that enabled attacking troops to enter the enemy's line, whilst preventing enemy troops from entering the attack area.

box open, box shut

Cigarettes were a much prized item in the trenches and soldiers habitually put their cigarettes into metal tins, as the fragile packets would be crushed.

If a man were offering his around, he would use this expression and only those nearest and quickest would be able to avail themselves of the offer. Officers tended to use cigarette cases. See also *fag, gasper*.

bracketing An artillery term for testing the range of a target by firing shots over and under, left and right of a target. When the shells bracketed it, the other guns in the battery would be given the same firing co-ordinates and a barrage would be unleashed. See also *registering*.

brads Cigarettes, generally Australian. See also *fag, gasper, nicky*. Other names for cigarettes included *coffin nails, dags, smoke*.

brag A popular card game generally said to have been named after Philip Bragg, the colonel of the 28th Regiment of Foot (the Gloucesters Regiment). He was said to have popularized the game in the mid-18th century.

brass hats General Staff, from the amount of gold wire on their hats. They were usually despised by the infantry, often unfairly.

brass monkeys, cold enough to freeze the balls off of Extremely cold. An Australianism not much recorded prior to the very late 19th century.

brassard

An armband showing that the wearer was a specialist, with the red cross on it or sometimes the letters SB to denote *stretcher bearers*, or MP for *Military Police*.

brassed off

Fed-up, a regular army expression possibly originating from the dull routine of cleaning one's brass insignia.

bread and jam

A tram.

breakthrough

A military tactic that required attacking troops to penetrate and hold a given point in the enemy's line. Every general dreamed of making a decisive breakthrough, but it seldom happened.

breamy, that's

A bad thing, as in 'They're organizing fatigues, that's breamy.'

breather, to take a

To have a rest, and catch one's breath.

breeze-up

To become scared. See also *wind-up*.

bride and groom

A broom.

brief, a

A 19th-century civilian word meaning a ticket of any sort, but by the 20th century it also meant in military terms a leave pass or discharge papers. See also *chit*.

brigade

A military formation nominally comprising 5,000 men made up of four infantry battalions and their attached support troops. See Appendix 2.

brigadier general	The officer commanding the brigade.
Bristol fighter	The Bristol F2b fighter/ reconnaissance aircraft. Often called the 'Brisfit'.
British warm	The issue army greatcoat, made of wool and reaching to the knee. It was warm, but in wet weather tended to become waterlogged and mud clung to it tenaciously.
Brock's benefit	The continual show of *Very lights* (flares) sent up by both sides at night. After John Brock, the famous fireworks manufacturer, who founded his company in Islington, London in 1728.
broody	Dull-witted, slow or slovenly.
brown bread	Dead.
brown hat	A cat.
Brownies	Female land workers, from their brown overalls.
BS	Predominantly a Canadian abbreviation for bull-shit.
BSA	Birmingham Small Arms, a large firearms manufacturer but also the supplier of motorcycles to the army. They were not known for their compliant suspension, and BSA soon came to mean 'bloody sore arse'.
bubbly	Champagne. A civilian expression from the late 1890s.
Buck	From *c.* 1880, the nickname for any man called Taylor, from a popular

cowboy in Buffalo Bill's Wild West Show.

Buckle A Jew, from the rhyming slang 'buckle my shoe'.

buckshee Free. Also known as 'backsheesh', 'backshee' or 'buckshee'. Taken from the Persian word 'bucksheesh', meaning a present. Commonplace by *c*. 1780 and brought to England by the regular army. Much used in the Great War, although an odd derivation used by New Zealand troops meant to receive a light wound.

buddoo An Arab, mostly used by troops serving in the Middle East. From the Arab word 'bedu' or 'bedouin'.

buddy A friend. An Americanism dating from the mid-19th century, it became widely used by the British soldiers. It has had a resurgence of use in the last couple of decades.

bugger Originally a 16th-century term for a thief who stole from drunks. In the south of England by the 17th century it had come to mean a sodomite and was often used to describe an unpleasant person. By the Great War, it had also become pejorative, relating to a disagreeable, dangerous or difficult task. 'Shifting those dud shells will be a bugger.'

First Contemptible. "D'you remember halting here on the retreat, George?"
Second ditto. "Can't call it to mind, somehow. Was it that little village in the wood there down by the river, or was it that place with the cathedral and all them factories?" (Punch)

bugger all	Meaning nothing, or of no consequence. 'Thought I was on a serious charge, but it was bugger all.'
bugger up	To destroy, ruin or spoil. 'Those *Minnies* didn't half bugger up the trench last night.'
bull ring	The infamous training establishment at *Etaples*, staffed mostly by non-combatant *base wallahs*. The cruel treatment inflicted on troops passing through, allied to its sandy nature, made a comparison with the Spanish bull ring inevitable. See also *canary*.
bullet up the spout	To have one's rifle loaded and ready to fire.

51

bullock's liver A river.

bully beef Corned beef. It was a staple part of the monotonous army diet and was made into stews, fried in slabs, eaten cold and often bartered with French civilians for something more appetizing.

Bumble Sometimes Bumble and Buck. Slang for the popular *Crown and Anchor* board game.

bumf Short for bum-fodder, any paper that could be used for toilet purposes. Derived from the mid-19th-century Wellington College tradition of a 'bumf-hunt' or paper chase, it had by 1914 also become a reference to the mountains of largely irrelevant military paperwork.

bump A near miss from a shell, from the impact it made. Often used as a verb. 'We got really bumped yesterday.'

bunce From the 18th-century word 'buns' meaning money or profit. By 1900 it meant to come into an unexpected windfall, often through gambling.

bunch up The tendency soldiers had during an attack to close up together, often with fatal results.

bund A Hindi word for a dam or embankment. Zillebeke Bund was a well-known example in Ypres.

bundle of ten Often simply 'bundle'. A pack of

cigarettes, adapted from the army
habit of issuing ten blankets in a
bundle. Popular with Australians.

bun-fight
A tea-party, but used in the army,
predominantly by officers, to describe
any fracas from a trench-raid to
fist-fight.

bunk with or bunk-mate
Originally a naval term it meant a
chum that you shared a sleeping
place (hammock or *funk hole*) with.
Also 'to do a bunk' which was to
depart rapidly, often when authority
arrived. An Americanism from the
mid-19th century.

Burberry
An officer's trench coat, also the town
of Burbure.

Burglars
Bulgarians, one of the four Central
Powers, which also included
Germany, Austria-Hungary and the
Ottoman Empire.

burgue or burgoo
Army oatmeal porridge. An old word
dating from at least the first half of
the 18th century. British soldiers
used the former pronunciation,
Australians the latter.

bus
Airforce slang for an aeroplane and a
naval term for a small boat.

bushel and peck
The neck.

Business
The town of Busnes.

butcher's
To have a look, from 'butcher's hook'.

butt-notcher
A sniper, from the habit some had of
notching the stock with each kill,

greatly discouraged by the army. If the sniper was captured it invited immediate death.

button-stick A flat brass plate with indentations and a slot in the centre, that allowed buttons, buckles etc to be cleaned without getting the polish onto clothing.

buzzer The Morse tapper used for sending telegraphic messages. Also 'to buzz' was to send a Morse message.

Byng-Boys Canadians, after the popular revue of the same name. Their commander was Julian Byng, later Viscount Byng of Vimy (1862–1935). Also a very popular stage revue.

C3 In the early years of the war, men were categorized in fitness for military service as A1, B2, B3, etc. C3 was the lowest category; wounded men were automatically given this category and they were often allocated garrison or base duties.

cable trench Quite literally a straight trench into which communication cables were laid.

cadre A core of officers and men kept back from an attack to provide a nucleus for the reformation of the unit afterwards. As some battalions could lose 80 per cent of their complement in a day, this was very necessary.

cagnas
A Canadian term for barracks, probably from the French word 'cagnat', a shelter.

Cain and Abel
A table.

cake-walk
An easy job. From the popular pre-war dance.

Camel
The Sopwith Camel fighter, introduced in early 1917.

Camel Corps
The Imperial Camel Corps, a unit formed to fight in desert conditions in 1916, but more frequently used as a derogatory term for the infantry.

Camellia
An Australianism for a member of the *Camel Corps*.

camouflage
A French word adopted into English. It meant the art of concealing oneself or position from enemy observation by whatever was the most effective means and it was pioneered in the army by painter Solomon J. Solomon, RA (1860–1927). It could be paint or material (*scrim*), and was used to cover any military object from observation. Camouflage became a vital part of the military's defence.

camouflet
From the medieval term 'moflet', it was a counter-mine used to destroy enemy mine galleries.

canary
An instructor at the *bull ring*, named after the yellow *brassard* on his arm.

cane
From the school expression 'caning', to receive a beating. It meant to be

shelled heavily or to suffer unduly. 'The emma-gees post got caned last night.'

canister or case shot
A naval shell, containing steel balls designed to take down rigging on ships. Later adapted to land use, by 1914 its normal form was as airburst shells. See also *shrapnel*.

canned or canned up
Tipsy or drunk.

cannon fodder
A derogatory term for soldiers who were regarded as simply expendable. It has its earliest origins in Shakespeare's 'Henry IV', Part 1, when Falstaff refers to men who were fit only as 'food for (gun) powder'. The actual term was first noted in print in 1814 by the French writer Françoise-Rene de Chateaubriand when he referred to army recruits being 'chair a canon' or cannon fodder.

canteen
The two-part tin pan carried by every soldier in which his rations were cooked. With a shallow top and deeper base, it was used to prepare everything – porridge, stew, soup, tea or rice – and to receive pre-cooked food from the cookhouse. There were also base canteens, where men could buy food, but these were few and far between. See also *dixie*.

canteen medals
Beer stains on a tunic.

cap comforter

A simple woollen tube that made a comfortable hat, or scarf. See also *balaclava cap*.

Cap off

An order given to a man on a disciplinary charge and appearing before his commanding officer, or court martial. The man was also prohibited from wearing a belt or side-arms.

Cape Hope

Soap.

Captain Cook

A book.

card

A man who was sharp-witted, funny or clever. Its origin is unclear but may derive from the mid-19th-century expression for a local character or rather odd fellow.

cards

A plural of the term *card* referring to a man (or men) of wit or cunning, as in 'They're a couple of cards, and no mistake.' Also one of the most popular pastimes among the soldiers, who played card games whenever possible, many of which were very ancient, 'All Fours' dating back at least to 1674. The list of games is almost endless: Card Bango, (later to become Bingo), Brag, Blind Man's Bluff, Pig, Indian Rummy and Kaiser, many of which were played for small amounts of cash, usually a franc. Clever players often made considerable amounts of money as a result.

carney
Devious, artful, but also used of flattery or persuasive language.

carpet slipper
A heavy shell, passing high above, from the whispering sound it made.

carrier pigeon
Much used in an age where radio communication was in its infancy. A message was attached to the bird's leg and it was released in the hope that it would reach its destination.

carrying party
See *ration party*, *working party*.

carving knife
Wife. Also known as *trouble and strife*.

castor oil merchant
A doctor.

catapult
Properly, the West Spring Gun, a near-medieval design using a spring-loaded arm to throw a grenade over the *parapet*, which it frequently failed to do.

caterpillar
A generic name for any tracked vehicle, though mostly the large tractors used to pull guns.

catsood
Drunk, from the French 'quatre-sou'd'.

cat-stabber
A bayonet or sometimes trench or jack-knife. See also *pin*.

catwalk
A brick pathway laid across fields to provide a drier pathway for soldiers. Of Great War origin.

CB
Confined to barracks, a fairly minor punishment.

CCS
A Casualty Clearing Station. Hutted or tented encampments just behind the front lines where men who had received initial treatment would then be classified as 'dangerous', 'slight' or 'evacuation' cases.

C'est la guerre
A French expression widely adopted to explain the vagaries of the war. Often said with a shrug.

CGM
Conspicuous Gallantry Medal. See Appendix 6.

chalk-farm
Arm.

char
Tea, from a Hindi word.

Charger
Pre-war, a cavalry horse, but latterly it referred to the five-round metal clip used for reloading rifle magazines.

Charley
The soldier's pack.

Charley Chaplin
The small moustache often worn by officers. It enabled German snipers to single them out and the fashion dwindled after 1915.

Charley Chaplin's Army Corps
The Canadian Casualty Assembly Centre at Shorncliffe in England. Predominantly used by Canadian troops.

Chasseurs
French light infantry or cavalry.

chatt
A louse. The derivation of this is much disputed. It may have come from the word 'chateren', recorded in the 13th century, and it was certainly in use in the 17th century as

referring to lice. Soldiers in the Napoleonic Wars used 'chatty' to mean lousy. The soldiers' habit of sitting around in groups to catch and kill them was, by the Great War, communally known as chatting.

check
To receive one's check was to obtain a military discharge.

cheer-o or cheerio
Although nowadays used as an expression when departing, it was originally a greeting used when either meeting or leaving, like the old Saxon 'wassail'. Originally used by officers it filtered through the ranks to become a universal term. See also *be good*, *chin-chin*, *toodle-pip*.

cherry nob
Military Policeman, from his red cap. See also *nit*, *Red Caps*.

chevron
The stripes on the arm of an NCO. Also known as *stripes*.

chew the fat
Originally a 19th-century expression meaning to be resentful or sulky, by 1914 it had come to mean to argue endlessly. See below.

chew the rag
This expression originally meant to argue endlessly. However, its use had dwindled by 1914 and *chew the fat* became the predominant expression for arguing.

chicken perch
A church.

china plate	Mate.
chin-chin	A farewell meaning 'be good', or 'be careful'. See also *be good*, *cheer-o*, *toodle-pip*.
chin-strap	To 'arrive on your chin-strap' meant to finish a march or task that left you utterly exhausted, kept upright only by your cap or helmet. In practical terms, the chin-strap of a steel helmet was meant to be worn under the chin, but a hard blow from a projectile could break the wearer's jaw or even his neck. Many men preferred to leave the strap looped over the brim, or hanging down at the back.
chin-wag	In the mid-19th century to be impertinent to someone in authority, but by 1914 a general term for any sort of casual conversation.
Chinese attack	A feint or diversionary attack.
Chinese whispers	Unsubstantiated rumours or half-truths. See also *clack*, *cookhouse rumour*, *furphy*.
Chink	Originally an Australianism for a Chinese labourer. Britain employed 140,000 on the Western Front, where they built roads, emptied ships, laid rail track and repaired machinery and tanks. Some 2,000 died in service.

chinny	Sugar, from a Hindi word.
chips	Originally an 18th-century naval word for a carpenter, it became 'chippy' and in the army was specifically applied to pioneer sergeants.
chit or chitty	A Hindi word for a paper. It referred to any message or note.
chloride of lime	Calcium hypochlorite powder, a form of powdered bleach, used for disinfecting latrine trenches and battlefield graves.
chokey	Prison, or a cell from the Hindi 'chauki', a four-sided building. See also *clink, cooler, coop, hutch, jug*.
chow	Food. Adapted from pidgin English and used more by American troops than British.
chronic	Very bad. From the medical term meaning a serious condition. It could be used as an adjective or adverb, 'That stew yesterday was chronic.'
chuck out one's dummy	To faint on parade.
chum	The most popular army term for a close comrade. See also *cobber, mate, pal*. A *long haired chum* was a girlfriend.
circus	The term applied to a flight of German fighter planes whose habit of circling allied aircraft was reminiscent of a circus arena. It was

particularly used in 1917 when Baron Manfred von Richthofen and his squadron were operating.

civvy
A civilian. It was used as an adjective or noun and 'civvies' were also civilian clothes.

clack
A rumour. Scottish, from the 16th century when it meant loud talk. See also *Chinese whispers*, *cookhouse rumour*, *furphy*.

click
Used when two people, usually male and female, had a mutual attraction. See also *get off*.

clickety-click
66, used in the game of *House*.

client for Rouen
A soldier with venereal disease. The hospital at Rouen was the normal destination.

clink
Prison or a cell, originally applied to the notorious Southwark gaol. From the sound of steel fetters. See also *chokey*, *cooler*, *coop*, *hutch*, *jug*.

clobber
Uniform or equipment, probably from a mid-19th-century Jewish term for used clothes.

clock
A face, as in 'clock-face'. Also to look at something. 'Clock that rum-jar over there.'

clothes pegs
Legs.

clutching hand, the
The quartermaster, who always seemed to demand that some or other personal item be replaced at a cost.

CO Commanding officer.

coal box A German shell of 5.9in or more, from the cloud of black smoke that it produced. See also *Black Maria*, *crump*, *Johnson or Jack Johnson*.

coal scuttle The German steel helmet. Although often ascribed to its shape, which was vaguely similar to a metal coal scuttle, the term was much used in the early 19th century to describe a poke bonnet.

coal-up Pay parade. Coal was thieves' slang for money in the 17th century and this logically transferred to the handing out of pay.

cobber A chum or mate, a popular Australianism. Possibly from the Yiddish 'chaber', a friend. See also *chum*, *digger*, *mate*, *pal*.

coffin nails Cigarettes. See *fag*, *gasper*, *nicky*. Other names for cigarettes included *brads*, *dags*, *smoke*.

cold, to have someone To have a person at a great disadvantage, or badly beaten. Probably American, *c.* 1830, from the boxing term 'out cold'.

cold feet Fear or cowardice.

cold meat ticket The soldier's identity disc.

cold storage A prison or cell. See also *chokey*, *clink*, *cooler*, *coop*, *hutch*, *jug*.

colney hatch A match. See also *lucifer*.

colour of the day Pre-arranged flare colours that

	changed on a daily basis to ask for artillery support.
Colt gun	A light machine-gun of .30in calibre, manufactured by the Colt Company of Hartford, Connecticut. See also *potato digger*.
column dodger	A man who shirked his duty.
come the old bag or soldier	To try to avoid work or wheedle oneself an easy job. Also to make a nuisance of oneself.
comforter	See *balaclava cap*.
comic business	A pilot's term for flying.
comic cuts	The weekly divisional intelligence summary. Seldom believed by the soldiers.
commo	A communication trench. Also known as *CT*.
company	A unit within a battalion of about 230 men at full strength. See Appendix 2.
complaints, Any?	The normal request made by the orderly sergeant about the quality of food. Making a complaint could earn the enmity of assorted NCOs and was usually unwise.
compree	Do you understand? From the French 'compris'.
comsah	A variant of the French 'comme ça', meaning 'like that'. Often used with a shrug, as in 'That shell wiped out the cooker comsah.'
concamp	Convalescent camp for wounded men.

concertina wire
Barbed or barbless wire that wrapped around an intruder if touched.

conk or conk out
A late war aviation term for an engine that had stopped working. Latterly applied to anything that didn't work.

conscientious objectors
These were men who for religious or pacifist reasons refused to fight. Many joined the medical services, and special 'Non-coms companies' were formed after March 1916 to provide labour in the front lines. Those who refused to enlist were imprisoned and often treated very harshly.

conscript
Also *draftee*, a man forcibly drafted into the army by the Military Service Act of 27 January 1916.

conshie
Shortened form of *conscientious objector*.

consolidate
To secure a position against counter-attack. Also used when trying to gain favour from a superior.

Contemptibles
See *Old Contemptibles*.

Continental News
A propaganda newspaper issued to British prisoners of war.

contour-chasing
Very low flying.

convoy
Ships or vehicles carrying supplies or soldiers.

coogage
A newspaper, from the Hindi word for paper.

cooker
The mobile field kitchen pulled by draft-animals. Company cooks prepared all hot meals, from porridge to roast meat and they were frequently close enough to the front lines to be shot at.

cookhouse rumour
Also 'cookhouse official' or *latrine rumour*. Rumour based on hearsay and partial information. Although often decried, soldiers frequently found out more about what was happening from the cookhouse than they ever did from official sources. See also *Chinese whispers, clack, furphy.*

Cook's tour
Official visits to the front by politicians, senior officers or the press. It took its name from the tour company of the same name, who were already well-established by 1914.

cooler
A military cell, from the American term to be imprisoned when drunk to cool off. See also *chokey, clink, coop, hutch, jug.*

coop
A cell. See also *chokey, clink, cooler, hutch, jug.*

coot or cooty
A louse, or lousy. Although a Cockney word, it was much used by ANZAC soldiers.

cop it, cop one or cop a packet
To be killed or wounded. 'Where's Jim? Oh, he copped it last night.' In its original early 18th-century form, it meant to be caught or captured by

	the authorities. As an aside, it was the derivation of the word 'coppers'.
cordite	A string-like propellant used in small arms ammunition and shells. When chewed it gave men the temporary symptoms of having a fever but few experienced medical officers were fooled.
corduroy road	See *plank road*, also *duckboard*.
corkscrew-stake	See *screw picket*.
corns and bunions	Onions.
Corp	Abbreviated form of 'Corporal'. Only used by those familiar to him.
corpse factory	A very successful piece of British propaganda that declared that Germany was reducing down corpses to make fat and soap.
corpse ticket	Identity disc.
corrugated iron	Also known as *expanded sheeting*. Thin metal sheeting used to support trench walls or *dug-out* roofs. See also *elephant iron*.
counter battery fire	Eliminating enemy artillery batteries.
course	An instructional period behind the lines where officers and men were periodically sent. This covered everything, from grenades to map-reading and sniping. Sometimes useful but mostly a subtle way of giving men who were war-weary a spell out of the lines.

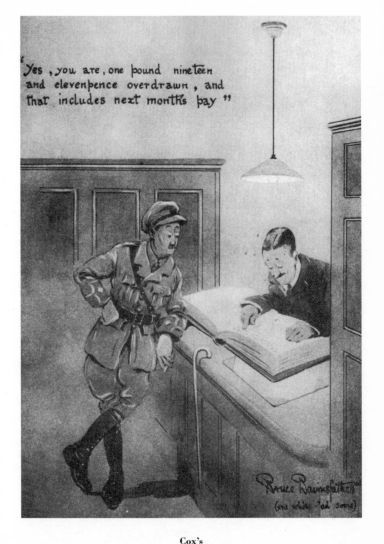

Cox's
When one feels rather in favour of floating a War Loan of one's own.
(Bruce Bairnsfather, author's collection)

covering party A protective line of riflemen in front of a working party.

cow or cow juice Milk, a Canadianism. Also, as an Australian expression, something that was bad or unfair. 'That shelling was a real cow.'

Cox and Co The predominant Bank of the Great War. Over 250,000 men were on their books by 1916 and 50,000 cheques were cleared a day. Almost all officers banked with Cox's.

Coxey's Army A rag-tag army. Predominantly Canadian, but from an American term referring to the march of the unemployed led by Jacob Coxey in 1894.

crab grenade Properly the M.1915 Discushandgranate, a disk-shaped grenade with projecting striker pins.

crab wallah A bad person; Indian Army expression.

crabs Body lice. See also *chatt*.

crap To defecate. It can be traced back to an English word used in the mid-18th century meaning to gather in a crop, but how its meaning altered is a mystery. Much used by American troops.

crappo A French *trench mortar*, 'une crapaud'.

crate A Royal Flying Corps word for an aeroplane.

crater
The hole left behind by a shell or mine.

crawling with
Originally referring to lice, its meaning widened to signify a large number of anything. 'It's fair crawling with Huns there.'

creased
To be knocked out or slightly wounded.

create
To make a fuss about something.

creeping barrage
The use of artillery to advance their fire at a pre-arranged speed, enabling the infantry to follow closely behind. Very difficult to organize effectively.

cricket ball
The British No. 28 grenade.

crime sheet
A written record of a soldier's misdemeanours and punishments.

croaker
A medical officer, from 'to croak', or die.

Croix de Guerre
A French award for gallantry, often given to British soldiers.

Crown, the
A sergeant major.

Crown and Anchor
A very popular board game that used dice and a cloth marked with squares. Bets were placed on the squares, in a similar manner to roulette. Betting for money was technically illegal in the army but this was seldom enforced. Always accompanied by a commentary. See *patter*.

Crucifix Corner
Any junction with a wayside calvary.

crucifixion
See *Field Punishment No. 1*.

crump   A large explosion from any sizeable shell.

CT   A communication trench.

cubby hole   A small *shelter* or shallow *dug-out*. See also *funk hole*.

cuffer   A lie or tall story. Popular in the army from *c.* 1870.

cumsah   An item that the speaker cannot put a proper name to. 'Hand me that cumsah will you?' From the French 'comme ça'. See also *ooja or oojah*, *wotsit*.

cup and a wad   Tea and a sandwich or bun.

curtain fire   Heavy shellfire between an enemy section of the line and our own. Often ued to prevent counter-attacks.

cushy   Also 'cooshy' or 'cushti'. Something safe, easy or undemanding. Its origin is disputed: it possibly comes from the Hindi 'khush', pleasurable; or Romany gypsy 'kushto', good; or French 'coucher', to lie down.

cut, to be   To be snubbed or ignored. From 'to be cut dead'.

cut up nasty or rough   In the early 19th century this meant to be quarrelsome or dangerous but by the 20th century it had come to mean badly treated or suffering unduly, originating from horseracing circles. In a military sense, a soldier might say 'The platoon was badly cut up in that attack.'

Cuthbert	A shirker or fit man not serving in the army.
DADOS	Deputy Director of Ordnance Services. There was one in every division.
dag up	To smarten up, from the farming term 'dagging' for shearing the hindquarters of sheep to keep them clean.
dags	Cigarettes. See also *fag, gasper, nicky*. Other names for cigarettes included *brads, coffin nails, smoke*.
Daily Mail	Tail.
daisy pusher	A man with a fatal wound.
daisy roots	Boots.
dam all	An expurgated form of fuck all (*FA*) or *bugger all*.
Dardanelles	The naval operation begun in February 1915 that led to the Gallipoli Campaign, a ten-month stalemate for the allied forces, who abandoned it in December 1915.
Darky	Anyone named Smith. From the fact that all village smiths were identifiable by their smoke-blackened faces. 'Smudger' was another common nickname for a smith.
DCM	Distinguished Conduct Medal. See Appendix 6. Also District Court Martial.
dead beat	Worn out. See also *beat, beaten to a frazzle, chin strap*.

dead nuts on	To be very enthusiastic about something or someone.
dead soldier	An empty beer bottle.
dead to the world	Fast asleep.
debus	To get out of an army lorry or bus.
Decauville railway	A narrow gauge railway (normally 1ft 11in) used to transport supplies, ammunition and wounded. Thousands of miles of track were laid across the front.
deep end, to go off the	To lose one's temper, often violently. A metaphor for the sudden explosion of water when one jumps into a swimming pool.
dekko	To have a look at. From the Hindi word 'dekhna', to see.
de-lousing station	A place where periodically men could exchange lice infected clothes for replacements that had been baked at high temperature so as to kill the vermin. It seldom did. See also *disinfector*.
demis	A term for convalescent wounded, from the French 'demi', half.
demo	A demonstration, usually of artillery who would bombard an enemy sector for no discernable reason.
demob	Demobilization, every soldier's dream.
depot	Regimental HQ.
Der Tag	Literally, the day. Used by Germans to describe the eventual defeat of the

	allies. Later facetiously to refer to when the war would end.
Derby Men	Lord Derby was Director General of Recruiting who introduced in October 1915 a scheme of deferred enlistment, prior to conscription being introduced. Men who volunteered returned to their jobs until called up.
derzey	The regimental tailor, from the Hindi word 'dhirzi'.
deuce and ace	Face.
devil-dodger	The chaplain.
Devil's Wood	Delville Wood on the Somme. The South African Brigade entered the wood with 3,033 officers and men and after six days of fighting left with 172 men and two officers. Now the National War Memorial for South Africa.
DFC	Distinguished Flying Cross. See Appendix 6.
DFM	Distinguished Flying Medal. See Appendix 6.
dial	The face, from clock dial.
dickey dirt	Shirt.
dido	Rum, a naval term whose derivation is unknown.
dig oneself in	To prepare a protective trench or shelter.
digger	Used by Australians as a generic term for any comrade. Originating in

the gold-fields to distinguish between stake-holders and squatters, it fell out of use but was revived in 1915, by Australians on Gallipoli who spent most of their time digging out soil to fill sandbags. See also *cobber*.

dingbat A *batman*, mostly Australian.

dingo Eccentric or crazy. Probably from the French 'dingot', or mad.

dinky A mule.

dinky-doo Number 22, from the game of *House*.

dippy Simple, foolish or slow. Probably from the medical 'dipsomania' for alcoholism, leaving a person confused and slow-witted. See also *doolally*, *tapped*, *touched*.

dirty work at the crossroad Originally meaning to have sex, but also used to indicate trouble or danger.

dish out To distribute something. It could refer to food, the award of medals or even heavy shelling. 'Fritz is really dishing it out tonight.'

disinfector The ovens used to bake clothing to kill lice. See also *de-lousing station*.

ditched, to be A pre-war American hobo expression meaning to be ejected from a moving train, often into a ditch. Later adopted to describe any vehicle that had become stuck in a ditch or trench, or was otherwise

	immobile. Particularly used by the Tank Corps post-1916.
division	An army unit of approximately 20,000 men. Commanded by a major general. See Appendix 2.
divvy	To divide up, but also an abbreviation for an army division.
dixie	Correctly, a large iron cooking pot in which hot food was cooked and from which it was served, but frequently used when referring to the soldier's small tin *canteen*. From the Indian word 'deschai'.
do, a bit of a	Used as a noun, it referred to an attack or raid, but it was also used as an expression for jollity. 'We're having a bit of a do in the estaminet tonight.'
do an alley	Leave quickly, from the French 'allez', to go.
do down	To swindle, an old English expression from the 17th century.
do in	To kill. Originally a criminal expression.
do one's bit	To join up and fight.
dobbs	Army pork, origin unknown.
dock	Hospital, from the naval term 'going into dock' for ship repairs.
doctor, the	A *No. 9* pill to purge the system.
dodger	A good conduct medal.
dodging the column	Avoiding any work or fatigues. Originally a cavalry expression from the Boer War (1899–02).

dog
To make a show of oneself, an Australianism.

dog and maggot
Biscuit and cheese, from 'dog's biscuits with maggots'.

dog fat
Butter.

dogfight
Arial combat between two or more aircraft.

dog's leg
A lance-corporal's stripe.

doings
Whatever is most pressing to be done at that moment. From the American expression for the ingredients of a meal, *c.* 1830.

Dolly
Anyone named Gray, from a popular song, 'Goodbye Dolly Gray'.

done in, done for or done up
Exhausted, worn out, finished. Said of a wounded man who is near death.

doo hickey
An airforce word for any small useful gadget. The Canadians preferred 'doo flicker'.

doolally or doolally tap
The literal meaning was to be mad with sunstroke and was from the Hindi word 'deolali'. It became much used to describe anyone who was not normal. See also *dippy*, *tapped*, *touched*.

door knob
A shilling, from the rhyming slang for 'bob', meaning 'knob'.

dooshman
Pre-1914 regular army word for an enemy. From a Hindi word.

dosh
A bivouac or *funk hole*, predominantly Canadian. It had no

connotation with money until well after the war.

dough
Money. Mostly an Americanism, dating from the mid-19th century.

doughboys
US soldiers, and their preferred nickname. Probably from the Mexican–American War (1846–48) where the marching men were covered in the local white dust, giving them the appearance of dough figures; also possibly from their similarity to the white adobe bricks commonly used.

down the line
Away from the front line, usually a safer place.

draft
A body of men selected from a base depot to provide reinforcements for a front-line unit.

draftee
See *conscript*.

dressing down
A telling-off for a minor offence. See also *on the mat*.

drum up
A navvy's expression for making tea by the roadside, from the Romany 'drom', or road. Used whenever or wherever soldiers' tea was required, which was mostly anytime.

drumfire
Concentrated artillery fire that sounded like a monstrous drum-roll.

DSC
Distinguished Service Cross. See Appendix 6.

DSM
Distinguished Service Medal. See Appendix 6.

DSO Distinguished Service Order. See Appendix 6.

dubbin An wax oil and tallow mix used to soften and waterproof leather, used since medieval times. When a piece of *four by two* rifle cleaning cloth was added to it, it made an ideal night lamp.

duckboard A ladder-like wooden flooring used to provide a solid surface in trenches or across boggy ground. Each was 8ft long and 2ft wide. They were heavy to move and often sank without trace in muddy ground. However they made excellent firewood. See also *plank road*.

duckboard slide or glide Losing your footing on wet and muddy duckboards. A common occurrence.

duckboard harrier A runner.

dud A shell that fails to explode. Also a soldier who is no good.

duff Pudding, especially plum or currant duff. Also an 18th-century word for goods that were inferior. During the war, used for anything that was bad or not up to standard. 'I've got a duff rifle.'

dug-out There were three types. The most sophisticated was a deep dug-out, reinforced with heavy timbers and accessed by wooden stairs. Some

German dug-outs were 60ft deep, with concrete stairs and pipes to bring fresh air in. There were at least two entrances, many larger German ones having four or more. They were lit by electric or oil lamps and contained stoves. The shelters were shallower with heavy *corrugated iron* (so-called *elephant iron*) roofing covered with sandbags, timber and earth. They would not stop a heavy shell but were reasonable protection from shrapnel and light artillery. *Cubby* or *funk holes* were shallow excavations in the *parapet* side of the trench just long and wide enough to take one or sometimes two men lying down. Timber to support the roof would be used if it could be *scrounged*, and a ground-sheet used to make it slightly more waterproof, but they were death traps in the event of a nearby shell burst as they would collapse onto the occupants. See also *funk hole*, *shelter*. Also used of an officer or NCO who was past retirement age but had returned to active service.

dug-out disease   A common psychological problem when soldiers proved reluctant to leave the safety of a shelter.

dug-out king   An officer or NCO who used his rank to ensure that he remained safely

The Dud Shell – Or the Fuse-Top Collector
Give it a good 'ard 'un Bert; you can generally 'ear 'em fizzing a bit first if they are a-goin'
to explode. (Bruce Bairnsfather, author's collection)

	underground. Sometimes called a 'dug-out warrior'.
Duke of Fife	Knife.
dulay and dupan	The nearest the British soldier could come to asking for milk, 'du lait', and bread, 'du pain'.
dumb insolence	Allowing an expression of boredom, amusement or derision on the face when being spoken to by a superior officer. It was a punishable offence.
dumdum	A soft-nosed or modified bullet designed to create the maximum damage. It was nick-named after the DumDum arsenal by soldiers serving in India, in part because Indian made ammunition was thought to be inferior. See also *tampered bullet*.
dummy	A fake head or figure created to deceive a sniper. Originating in the French Army, they could prove very useful in determining where a sniper was hidden.
dummy trenches	Fake trenches dug to fool enemy observers.
dump	An open area behind the lines where stores such as *trench mortars*, ammunition or timber were piled. After the civilian word for a rubbish-heap.
duration	An unspecified period that terminated at the end of the war. Most men signed up 'for the

duration'. A common toast when out of the line was 'Roll on the duration.'

Dusty
Men named Miller, because the miller was always coated in a fine layer of flour dust.

E
The letter scrawled on the medical label of a casualty, meaning that he was to be evacuated to England.

earn
A euphemism for 'to steal'. See also *found*, *scrounge*, *win*.

ears, to get one's put back
To have a haircut.

easy
'Stand easy' was an order to relax when on parade.

Eat apples
See *Etaples*.

echelon
Officially a formation of troops in parallel divisions.

Eeepray or Eeeps
The town of Ypres in Belgium. See also *Wipers*, *Ypres*.

egg and chips
Undoubtedly the most popular dish for soldiers out of the line. Almost all cafes and estaminets sold it, as well as many private houses. It appears to be a wartime invention due to the difficulty of finding meat. It was both cheap and nourishing and is still widely available in England today, though usually with sausages attached.

egg grenade
The British No. 16 grenade, but also the German Eierhandgranate M.1917.

Egypt Bread, regular army slang. Possibly from the biblical 'corn in Egypt'.

Egyptian Labour Corps Mostly used in the Middle East for the native labourers but sometimes applied derisively to the Army Service Corps.

elephant A semi-circular hut constructed of curved *corrugated iron*. Also a much heavier form of *corrugated iron* that was used for *dug-outs*, called *elephant iron*. This had a drilled central metal seam that could be bolted to another sheet to form a solid half-circle.

elephant iron See *elephant*.

embus To get on an army bus or lorry.

emergency rations Carried in the haversack, this comprised bully beef, biscuits, tea and sugar. It was only to be eaten in an emergency. Also called *iron rations*.

Emma A common German nickname for a large artillery piece. See also *Bertha*.

Emma Gee (MG) The shortened form of 'machine gun', more often used to describe members of the Machine Gun Corps.

Emma Pip (MP) Military Policeman.

emplacement A more or less permanent firing position for a machine gun or artillery piece.

enfilade To sweep with fire along the longest axis of an enemy formation. Machine guns were set up to enfilade enemy lines, so that advancing troops had to walk through a line of bullets coming not from directly ahead, but from left and/or right flanks.

entanglements   Barbed wire defences in front of a trench system, designed to entangle an enemy. Unless cut by artillery, they were normally impenetrable.

entrance fee   Just enough money to buy one drink.

Epsom races   Braces.

'Erb   A Cockney word for a joker or wag, probably from Herbert, a popular music-hall comedy name.

erfs   Eggs, 'oeufs'. Sometimes 'oofs'.

ersatz   Reserve or secondary. Used for second-line German infantry, but also increasingly applied to foodstuff supplied to German civilians that contained cheap additives, i.e. bread mixed with sawdust and coffee made from acorns.

estaminet   A French or Belgian café that was a mix of bar, pub and restaurant. Usually small with the barest of wooden tables and chairs and warmed by a huge iron stove. They were almost exclusively run by 'madame' often aided by her attractive daughters and this gave rise to much good-natured ribald conversation in pidgin French. Anything edible or drinkable could usually be bought; soup, eggs and chips, wine, beer. They provided warmth, good cheer, amusement and company for men out of the line and were fondly remembered by all veterans.

Esses Emma (SM) The sergeant major.

Etaples Normally pronounced 'Eat Apples'. A town 18 miles south of Boulogne where huge infantry depots and hospitals were situated. Conditions were unnecessarily harsh and a mutiny broke out in 1917 after serious abuses by the *Military Police*. It has one of the largest military cemeteries in France, with almost 11,000 burials.

evacuated, to be To be returned to the UK. See *E*.

evaporated vegetables Tasteless, soggy and unpalatable tinned boiled vegetables provided as rations. Seldom issued post-1915.

expanded sheeting See *corrugated iron*.

Eyeties Also 'Ityies'. Italians.

eye-wash Verbal deceit or empty threats. For the soldiers, official communiqués were 'eye-wash', as were warnings of dire punishment by junior officers for minor offences.

FA An abbreviation of 'fuck all'. Sometimes bowdlerized into 'Sweet Fanny Adams'. Also commonly 'Sweet FA'.

fag

A cigarette. Its origin is unclear but 'fagge' was an early English word meaning to droop or hang listlessly. This may have been subsequently adopted to describe a cigarette hanging on the bottom lip. Before the First World War it referred to any poor-quality cigarette, but from *c.* 1915 it meant virtually any type of cigarette. See also *gasper*, *nicky*, *Woodbine*. Other names for cigarettes included *brads*, *coffin nails*, *dags*, *smoke*.

fag-end

The butt of a cigarette. From the 19th century term for a rubbish collector, a 'fag-end man'.

faggot

A meatball, usually dished out behind the lines at field kitchens and usually made of bully beef and flour.

fair dinkum

Fair, honest or correct. Although an Australian term, it was a well recorded Lincolnshire expression of the mid-19th century meaning fair play or to have a fair share of work.

fair do

Also 'fair do's'. Something that was fair or just. 'Divvy out that loaf equally, fair-do's for all.' Much used by Australians but recorded as a Yorkshire expression from *c.* 1880's.

fairy light

A variation of *Very light*.

fantassins

The French soldier's word for the infantry, it originated from the

	medieval Italian 'fantaccino', young soldier. *PBI* was the British equivalent.
Fanny Adams	See *FA*.
Fanny Durack	Born in Sydney, Australia, from 1910–18 she was the world's greatest female swimmer. When the statue of Mary and the infant Jesus on the top of the Notre-Dame de Brebières basilica in Albert was knocked from the vertical by a shell, Australian troops nicknamed her 'Fanny' as she resembled the swimmer diving off the starting blocks. See also the *Leaning Virgin*.
fanti	Crazy or mad. From the Hindi for mad.
FANY	First Aid Nursing Yeomanry.
fascines	Large bundles of tightly compressed wooden branches held by chains. They were carried by tanks and dropped into enemy trenches to aid in crossing them. Each could weigh several tons.
fashy	Angry, from the French 'fâshé'. Usually directed at military incompetence. Primarily a New Zealand expression.
fatigue	Military chore. These included any form of manual labour, carrying rations, timber or barbed wire up to the lines, peeling potatoes or

repairing damaged trenches. Only machine gunners, snipers or sentries were excused.

fatigue dress Working uniform, with no belts, puttees or arms.

fattening up Abbreviation of 'fattening up for the slaughter'. A cynical expression used when units were taken out of the line for a 'rest'.

FDS Field dressing station. After the regimental aid post, the nearest point at which men could receive medical attention.

fed up An abbreviated form of 'fed up to the back teeth'. Tired out, bored or frustrated, first recorded during the Boer War. The full expression commonly used in the Great War was 'fed up, fucked-off and far from home'.

feel to your right A command for units on roads to close their ranks to permit other traffic to pass.

feeling out Artillery searching for a hidden target.

female See *tank*.

Fern Leaves or Ferns New Zealanders, from the fern motif on their badges.

fiddler Bizarrely, regular army slang for a bugler.

field cashier Army paymaster.

field dressing Two bandages were carried inside the tunic for immediate first-aid. One,

	the *field dressing,* was small, and the larger was a *shell dressing*. Soldiers used both terms randomly.
field grey	The grey-green colour used for German service uniforms and equipment.
field gun	A small artillery piece firing a 13lb, 18lb or 60lb shell.
Field Punishment No. 1	Also known as *crucifixion*, it required a man to be tied by hands and feet for two hours a day, and up to 90 days duration, to a fixed object such as fence or wagon wheel. It was very uncomfortable and humiliating.
Field Punishment No. 2	A soldier would be shackled by hands and feet for up to two hours a day, but was permitted to move about.
field service postcard	A pre-printed card on which the sender had to cross out the irrelevant parts. They did not require censoring and could be sent from France and be received in the UK the following day.
fighting order	See *battle order*.
fini or finee	Finished, ended or dead. From the French 'finis'. 'The sooner this war is fini the better.' See also *fini kaput*.
fini kaput	A curious mix of French and German, 'finis' and 'kaput', used by Germans to signify they were surrendering but often also by the British to signify the end of something.

fire alarms   Arms.

fire bay   A forward facing curve in a trench, protected on either side by earth and sandbags (traverses), from which a clear view of the enemy lines could be had. See also *traverse, trench*.

fire bucket   A coal or coke brazier.

fire step   The ledge cut into the lower forward side of a trench, so that a man could stand on it and look over the *parapet*.

fire trench   The front-line trench, containing *fire bays* from where men could shoot at the enemy.

firing squad   A squad (usually six men) detailed to execute a prisoner. An unpopular job, particularly if the shots failed to kill. The assistant provost marshal then had to administer the 'coup de grace' with a revolver.

five nine   A 5.9in shell.

fixed rifle   A rifle set up in a frame or clamp and aimed at an exposed point in the enemy's trench. Often very effective.

flag-wagger   A signaller.

flaming onions   A German 37mm quick-firing gun that used a tracer compound to track the projectile. So called because they flew upwards in long strings.

Flammenwerfer   Flamethrower. Introduced by the Germans on 26 February 1915, it comprised a pressurized tank of nitrogen and tank of liquid fuel,

(Image courtesy of Peter Smith)

normally petrol with a thickening agent. It was fed through a tube and projector nozzle and could fire a jet of flame between 160 and 250ft. It was deadly against *dug-outs*, bunkers and emplacements. Flamethrower operators were seldom taken prisoner.

flapper   An *Ayrton fan* but also a young woman of loose morals or sometimes a prostitute. The use of the word to describe a fashionable girl-about-town did not become commonplace until the 1920s.

flapper's delight   A young subaltern, self-explanatory!

flare pistol   A large-barrelled single shot pistol firing a brightly coloured flare to illuminate the ground or give a pre-arranged signal. See *Very pistol*.

flash   A patch worn on the shoulder to denote a specific division or battalion.

flea-bag   An officer's sleeping bag, although other ranks often made their own from army blankets.

flechette   See *aerial dart*.

flight   A flying unit of five or six aircraft.

flip   A pre-war flying expression denoting a short flight.

flog   To sell army property illegally. By 1918 it meant to sell anything.

fly slicer   Originally an 18th-century expression for a Life Guardsman, but

	by 1914 referred to any cavalryman, because of their swords.
flying arsehole	The flying observer's badge, with its large winged 'O'.
flying bedstead	A military bicycle or motorcycle. See also *jigger*.
Flying Circus	Specifically Jagdgeschwader 1 (JG 1) set up in June 1917 and commanded by Baron Manfred von Richthofen. The name came from its use of temporary and improvised landing fields, where tents were set up to provide shelter and accommodation.
flying pig	A 9.45in British heavy *trench mortar*.
Fokker	Named after the Dutch inventor Antony Fokker, these were a range of German fighter aircraft of superior performance. Often used by the British as a generic term for any enemy aeroplanes.
football	The 60-pdr or 2in medium mortar. Also known as a *plum pudding* or *toffee apple*. Spectacularly useless and prone to failing to detonate, it was replaced by the far more efficient *Stokes mortar*.
foot-slogger	An infantryman, regular army from the 1890s.
for it	In trouble, about to be punished.
forced march	A route march that required a great distance to be covered quickly. Units were known to cover 20 miles in a

day, a feat that would leave the men exhausted and with bloody feet.

Foreign Legion   The French Foreign Legion formed in 1831 and made up of all nationalities, with a deservedly tough reputation.

found   Usually a euphemism for stolen. See also *scrounge*.

four by two   A roll of flannel, each piece being nominally 4in x 2in, used for cleaning the barrel of a rifle or machine gun.

four letter man   Literally 'a shit'. In less graphic terms, a man who was of bad character.

Four Two   A 4.2in shell.

FP No. 1   See *Field Punishment No. 1.*

FP No. 2   See *Field Punishment No. 2.*

France and Spain   Rain.

fraternize   To mix with the enemy. The best publicized example was the 1914 Christmas truce. It was strictly against orders.

Fray Bentos   The premier brand of *bully beef* but often used to describe any issue tinned meat.

Fred Karno's Army   Frederick Westcott Karno (1866–1941) was a music-hall performer who invented slapstick comedy. His universal silliness was applied by soldiers to the running of the war in general and the army in particular.

friendly
A passing shell, regardless of whether it was 'ours' or 'theirs'.

frightfulness
Used widely by officers to describe any form of German activity, but also military stupidity in general.

frigo
Frozen meat, from the French 'viande frigorifiée'.

Fritz
A diminutive of Friedrich, used to describe German soldiers generically. See also *Boche*, *Hun*, *Jerry*, *Squarehead*.

frog and toad
Road.

frog it
To march or walk.

Froggie or Frog
French soldiers, from 'Frogs', a civilian slang term dating from the 1870s as a result of the mistaken belief that all Frenchmen ate frogs' legs. A 'frog' was also the belt-hanging strap for a bayonet or sword.

Front, the
The line that stretched from Nieuport on the coast to the Swiss border, a little over 450 miles. The British front covered some 70 miles from Flanders to the River Somme. To the soldiers, 'the front' comprised the forward area under direct enemy fire. Anywhere else was 'behind the lines'.

frying pan
The hand.

funk hole
A shallow excavation cut into the side of a trench. Certainly in use during the Boer War, it became a

common expression during the First World War for any form of *dug-out*. See *dug-out*, *shelter*.

funk, in a blue   Scared or terrified, often shortened to just 'funk'.

Funky Villas   The village of Fonquevillers, adjacent to Gommecourt, the most northerly point of the Somme offensive.

furlough   Leave, more commonly used by American troops.

furphy   Lie or half-truth, an Australianism taken from the name of Mr Furphy, who had the rubbish removal contract at the army barracks in Melbourne. See also *Chinese whispers*, *clack*, *cookhouse rumour*.

G & Q   General Duties and Quartermaster's Department. The staff who dealt, at divisional or higher levels, with the supply of matériel to the troops.

gadget   Any mechanical device, originally a naval term.

gaff   A small raid or attack, often pointless and costly. Post-war it became used to mean an error.

gallows   The wooden frame upon which straw dummies were hung for bayonet practice.

gambardier   An artilleryman in the Royal Garrison Artillery, responsible for the very large-calibre guns.

game

An event that was nonsensical or foolish. 'This raid tonight is a real game.' Also an Australianism, meaning stout-hearted, determined or brave.

gangway for a naval officer

Usually said quietly when a senior army officer was making his way through a mass of soldiers.

gas

A generic term for any poison gas. Although exposure to it was not always fatal, it was greatly feared by the soldiers on all sides. The first recorded use of gas was by the French in August 1914, who used a non-lethal teargas contained in grenades. It was used by the Germans in October 1914, at Neuve Chappelle, but it passed unnoticed. The first effective and lethal release of gas (Chlorine) on the Western Front was by the Germans on 22 April 1915, to which allied troops had no defence. In total 1.25 million men were affected by gas, of whom about 10 per cent died during the war and an unrecorded number subsequently died from the effects, often many years later.

gas alarm

A shell-case hung up and struck with a bayonet. Sometimes a football rattle or post-1917 most likely the more audible klaxon horn.

gas alert When the gas-mask was carried in a readiness position, to be put on at short notice.

gas bag The cloth bag that carried the gas mask. Leaving it behind was a punishable offence. Also an observation balloon or pompous officer.

gas cylinder A pressurized cylinder about 6ft long containing poison gas.

gas gangrene Myonecrosis, a deep muscle and tissue infection, caused by soil-borne bacteria entering a wound, causing the flesh to putrefy. With crude sterilization methods and no available treatment the end result was either amputation or death.

gas guard The man responsible for warning of an impending gas attack.

gas mask Primitive gas masks were cloth masks soaked in neutralizing chemicals. By the end of the war sophisticated rubber gas masks using charcoal filters were widely in use. Sometimes unofficially called a 'gasporator'.

gas projector Invented by Captain W.H. Livens, it was an 8in tube firing a 30lb gas cylinder up to 1,600 yards. Also known as a 'Livens Projector'.

gas sheet A rubberized sheet hung at the entrance to *dug-outs* or *pill boxes* to

	prevent the ingress of gas. See *waterproof sheet*.
gashio	Extra, additional, spare. A late 19th-century naval word, adopted by the army and subsequently shorted to 'gash'. 'Any gash stew left?'
gasper	The cheapest of cigarettes, normally an officers' term. See also *brads*, *fag*, *nicky*. Other names for cigarettes included *coffin nails*, *dags*, *smoke*.
gassed	Drunk.
gear	A soldier's personal equipment.
Geese	The Portuguese, Britain's oldest military allies. See also *pork and beans*.
German bands	Hands.
get away with it	A pre-war American expression meaning to escape punishment for a crime or misdeed.
get off	To be attracted to someone. Similar to *click*.
gippo	Regular army word for gravy, fat dripping or sometimes butter. Originally a mid-19th-century naval term. In the army it often meant fat, a favourite for dipping bread in. Also known as 'jippo'.
go over	To go into an attack. From the act of climbing over the *parapet*. See also *over the bags or over the top*.
go up	To head up to the front line.

going An abbreviated form of 'going spare', as in 'Is there any bully going?'

gold stripes Introduced in 1916, they were gold wound chevrons worn on the lower left sleeve, one for each time the wearer was wounded. See *wound stripe*.

gone dis Crazy, or mad. From the signallers' 'gone disconnected' meaning out of communication.

gone phutt From the Hindi word 'phatna', to explode. It meant something that had ceased to work, or was no longer in a fit state to be used.

gong A medal.

goo wallah The sanitary man.

goody-la Good. Used by the Chinese Labour Corps and generally adopted by British soldiers.

gorblimey Originally a Cockney corruption of 'God blind me', by the late 19th century it was used to denote a flat cap, often worn tilted over one ear. In 1914 it referred to the field service cap with earflaps, but as these ceased to be issued it became a general term for any peaked cap with the wire removed from the crown, to give it a rakish, well-used look, often favoured by young subalterns.

Gotha A large twin-engined German bomber introduced in 1917.

graft

Manual labour, a term first used in print in New Zealand in 1878. Widely used also in Australia and then adopted by the United States, where the expression referred more to illicit gain, or corruption.

Granny

The nickname for a series of British howitzers. Also 'Mother', 'Grandmother' and 'Great Grandmother', which were all very large howitzers of 9in, 12in and 15in calibres.

grass cutters

Small aerial bombs that spread *shell splinters* across a wide area.

Great or Big Push

The British offensive on the Somme, begun on 1 July 1916.

green cross shell

A German lachrymatory gas shell, from the markings painted on it. See also *blue cross shell*, *yellow cross shell*.

green envelope

An envelope that contained a letter whose contents were not subject to military censorship. The sender had to sign a declaration that there was nothing of military value therein.

grenade

A small hand-thrown bomb that used a time fuse. First invented in the mid-15th century, probably by the Spanish, as the name is a corruption of the city name Grenada. There were dozens of types, some more dangerous to the user than the enemy. See also *egg grenade*, *Mills grenade*, *stick grenade*.

greyback   The issue grey flannel shirt and also the grey-backed louse. See also *little grey home in the west*.

ground flare   A flare lit by attacking troops to show the limit of an advance.

ground stunt   Airforce slang for any activity near ground level, i.e. strafing enemy positions.

ground wallah   A non-flying airman.

grouse   To complain. A regular army expression whose origin is unclear.

grub stake   Rations, borrowed from the American mining expression.

GS   General Service, applied to any military item, from a tunic to a tank.

GS hairy, a   A military horse or mule. See also *long eared chum*.

guard room   The guard's office, the place a prisoner was taken to.

gumboots   Military calf-length rubber boots issued in particularly wet conditions. They proved inadequate for the deep mud so were replaced by a longer over-boot. See also *trench waders*.

gun bus   The Vickers FB5, a two-seater 'pusher' introduced in February 1915.

gun limber   Usually a 13- or 18-pdr light artillery piece, pulled by four horses with a

	detachable two-wheeled limber holding the ammunition. See also *limber*.
guncotton	Nitrocellulose made by combining nitrating cellulose and nitric acid. It generates six times the propellant gas of black powder and was ideal for use as an artillery propellant.
gunfire	Tea, usually the first early-morning brew. This reference may have derived from the green tea known as gunpowder (because that was what it resembled) favoured in India in the late 19th century and 'gunfire' may have arisen through analogy.
gunpowder or black powder	This was extensively used as a bursting charge in shrapnel and some smaller shells, but it is a deflagrate or low explosive and generally not effective in large shells. See also *HE*.
gutter crawl	A march through any built-up area.
guy	Originally a late 19th-century American word for a man, fellow or chap, it was often used by US troops to refer to each other.
HAC	The Honourable Artillery Company, who, oddly, were not artillerymen, but infantry. They were incorporated by Royal Charter in 1537, making them the oldest military unit in Great Britain.

hair brush The Grenade No. 12, a crude and very early British grenade, from its odd shape.

Hairpin, the British defensive sector near the infamous Hohenzollern Redoubt.

half a mo' A predominantly Cockney word for a cigarette.

half dollar Collar.

half-baked Daft, silly. Recorded as a Cornish expression in the mid-1840s and not an American expression as often thought.

half-inch To pinch, or steal. See also *pinch*, *scrounge*, *snaffle*, *win*.

Hales bomb A rifle grenade invented by Martin Hale in 1907 and adopted by Britain in 1915. A series of types followed, Nos. 3, 20, 24 and 35, which saw service until 1918. Despite being a grenade, they were oddly always referred to as bombs.

hand-cart cavalry The *Stokes mortar* section, also sometimes the *Lewis gun* section.

Hans Wurst The German equivalent of *Tommy*. They also called themselves Dreckfresser, mud-eater; Frontschwein, foot-slogger; Fusslatsche, Line-hog amongst others.

Happy Valley A narrow valley that saw much fighting on the Somme in late 1916.

hard tack	Naval term for ship's biscuits, also issued to the army.
harkers	Soldiers in a listening post. From the old English word to listen, 'hark'.
harness	The infantryman's webbing or leather equipment, from the analogy with horse harness.
Harry Randle	A handle. He was a popular music-hall artist pre-war.
Harry Tate	The Royal Aircraft Factory 'RE8' two-seater reconnaissance and bomber aircraft. First introduced in the summer of 1916, it was slow and vulnerable. Also rhyming slang for a plate. Tate was a music-hall comedian.
hate	A heavy bombardment, named after the infamous German *Hymn Of Hate*.
haversack	The small canvas or linen bag worn on the left side originally to carry 'havercake' rations, a simple biscuit of oats, water and salt. During the First World War it contained daily rations and a soldier's personal possessions. Sometimes confused with the large pack worn on the back.
Hazybrook	The town of Hazebrouck.
HE	High explosive. HE explodes instantly and very violently. There were many mixtures based around TNT and also ammonium nitrates, which as an additive which was cheaper than TNT.

heads, the

A popular term among soldiers who regarded themselves as a cut above the rest; its origin is obscure but it may refer to the head of the monarch on a coin. See also *knuts*.

heavy, a

A large artillery piece, usually firing a shell in excess of 5in diameter.

Heine or Heinie

A mostly American term for a German.

heliograph

A signalling mirror.

Hellfire Corner

The very dangerous spot on the Menin Road that was constantly targeted by German artillery.

high jump, for the

Due to be punished for some misdemeanour. See also *dressing down, on the mat*.

high velocity

See *whizz-bang*.

Hill 60, 63 etc

A rise in the ground that corresponded to its height above sea level in metres. Hill 60 near Ypres was one of the most infamous.

Hindenburg Line

A formidable defensive line constructed between 1916 and 1917 stretching from Arras to Soissons.

hipe

A rifle. Originating from the drill commands shouted on the parade ground. 'Order arms' was usually bellowed out as 'ordah hipe' or just 'hipe' and the mispronunciation stuck.

hitchy-koo

Itchy from lice bites. From the popular 'hitchy-koo' music hall

America in France
"I know we're fightin' for Democracy, but next time the Colonel comes around, salute, you
– son of a –!" (Bruce Bairnsfather, author's collection)

refrain written by Cole Porter when in Paris in 1917.

hoick   To pull up sharply, a flying term.

Hommes Forty (Hom Forty)   All French railway goods wagons were marked 'Hommes 40 ou Chevaux 8' (40 Men or 8 Horses) and it was generally agreed that the men suffered the greater discomfort.

honey bucket   Latrine bucket.

hooch   Alcohol, mostly used by American and Canadians. It comes from the Inuit word for spirit, 'hoocheno'.

hooha   A noise, hubbub or argument. Regular army.

hook, to sling one's   To move on or leave, usually after being told to do so. An 18th century term from the naval act of lifting an ancher to get underway.

hoop, jump through the   To be made to complete an unpleasant task, or be in trouble or simply to have to do something difficult. A circus expression.

hop over   An attack, from the act of jumping over the *parapet* or wire. See also *over the bags or over the top*.

horse lines   Where horses were tethered, a very vulnerable place as they were often within range of enemy guns.

hot   A double meaning, referring either to a dangerous part of the line, or to a woman who was regarded as amorous. See also *hot stuff*.

hot air	Boastful talk, rumour, baseles threats. Of American origin and popular with US troops.
hot stuff	A woman with relaxed sexual morals, but not a prostitute. Many British soldiers were puzzled by French women's apparent willingness to accept sexual advances, which was not the norm in England. The expression also came to mean someone who was very accomplished. 'He's hot stuff on that piano.'
Hotchkiss	A light machine gun used by British, French and American troops. Also the heavy QF 6-pdr guns used in British tanks.
House	One of the soldier's favourite games, using 15 different numbers which were called out; the winner was the first to shout 'House'. Now better known as Bingo. It came with a fast, amusing patter from the dealer.
housewife or hussif	A small pouch containing needle, thread, wool, buttons etc for immediate repairs.
how	Abbreviated form of howitzer. These were large-calibre short-barrelled guns that fired shells at a very high angle, giving them terrific penetrative power particularly against fortifications or *dug-outs*.

How's your father A meaningless expression taken from a popular music hall song that after 1915 became a hugely popular catchphrase. At least one officer, dying of wounds, was heard to use it as his last spoken words.

huffed From the game of draughts, where one counter is taken by another. A flying term meaning to be killed, usually by a fall (or jump) from a burning aircraft. Later adopted as a general term for being killed.

hump To carry, possibly from the use of camels as load-bearers in the outback. Mostly used by Australian troops.

Hun A German. The term originated from a Belgian newspaper article comparing the German invasion with that of the Huns from east of the Volga who had invaded the Roman Empire by AD 370. See also *Boche*, *Fritz*, *Jerry*, *Squarehead*.

Hunland Enemy territory; an airforce expression.

Hun-pinching A raid to capture an enemy soldier or patrol.

Hush-hush, the The Secret Service. Also 'The Hush-hush Crowd', members of the neophyte Tank Corps, whose existence in early 1916 was a very closely kept secret.

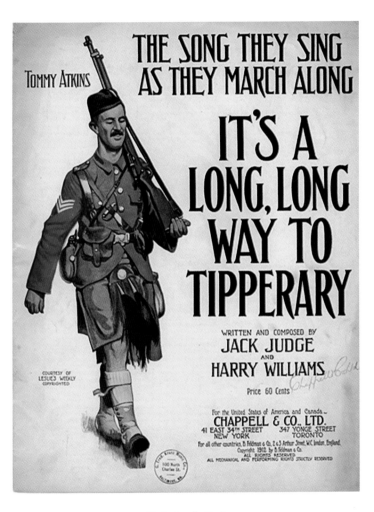

(Author's collection)

The Incorrigibles Again.

"What-ho, Charlie! Bit showery, ain't it?" (Punch)

"Wonder 'ow the Navy's getting on."

"Dunno. Ain't seen 'em about lately." (Punch)

And a Few Other Things

Napoleon said: "Every soldier carries a field marshal's bâton in his knapsack"

(Bruce Bairnsfather, author's collection)

THE HISTORY OF A PAIR OF MITTENS.

(Punch)

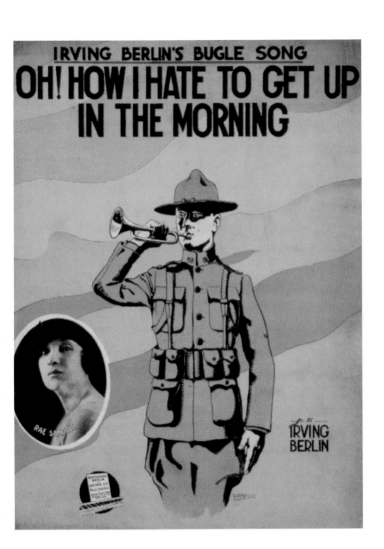

(Topfoto)

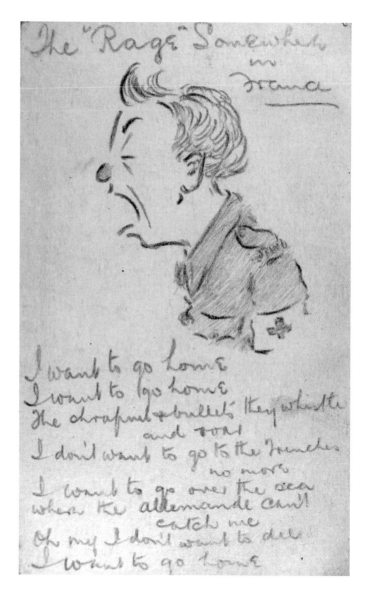

(Mary Evans)

Happy Memories of the Zoo

"What time do they Feed the Sea-Lions, Alf?" (Bruce Bairnsfather, author's collection)

THE DANCE OF DEATH.

The Kaiser. "STOP! STOP! I'M TIRED."
Death. "I STARTED AT YOUR BIDDING; I STOP WHEN I CHOOSE."

(Punch)

Vague Tommy (writing letter). "Wot day is it?" *Chorus.* "The fourteenth."

Tommy. "Wot month?" *Chorus.* "October."

Tommy. "Wot year?"

(Punch)

(Bruce Bairnsfather, author's collection)

As Between Friends.

British Lion: "Please don't look at me like that, Sam. *You*'re not the Eagle I'm up against." (Punch)

"Tommy" (*home from the front, to disaffected Workman*). "What'ld you think o' me, mate, if I struck for extra pay in the middle of an action? Well, that's what *you*'ve been doing." (Punch)

Awe-struck Tommy (from the trenches). "Look, Bill – Soldiers!" (Punch)

Modern Topography

" Well, you see, here's the church and there's the post-office "

(Bruce Bairnsfather, author's collection)

Hush-hush operation, the	A 1916–17 plan to put troops on the Belgian coast by amphibious landing. It came to nothing.
hutch	Guard room, cells, prison. See *chokey*, *clink*, *cooler*, *coop*, *jug*.
hutment	A camp of wooden huts or sometimes tents. They were cheerless places, bitterly cold and forlorn in winter, thick with mud in wet weather and dusty and wind-swept in summer, and usually close enough to the front to be shelled.
Hymn Of Hate	Written by Ernest Lissauer (1882–1937) in 1914 as a piece of jingoistic propaganda against Britain. It became a standing joke with the British Army, who referred to the German barrages as 'the daily hate'. For the lyrics, see Appendix 3.
'I'	The intelligence staff at HQ.
iddy-umpty	Dot and dash in Morse code, but sometimes a signaller.
identity disc	Up to late 1916 one composite fibre disc was worn, but thereafter two were issued, one red, one green. The red was removed from the body and returned to next-of-kin, the green remained with it, making subsequent identification easier. Many men wore privately

purchased or home-made metal discs on their wrists.

iggry To hurry up, quickly. From the Arabic 'iggri'. A much-shelled crossroads at Bullecourt was named Iggry Corner by the Australians. See also *jildi*.

improperly dressed A punishable military crime that could simply mean having an unfastened button.

imshi Go away, be off. From an Arabic word.

in the pink In good health or spirits. Probably the most commonly used phrase in letters home.

Ips One of several transliterations for the town of Ypres in Belgium. See also *Eeepray or Eeeps*, *Wipers*.

Irks (Erks) RAF air mechanics.

iron and brass A leave pass.

iron foundry Heavy shelling.

iron rations See *emergency rations*. Also the name of a famous Mk IV tank.

issue Anything that was government supplied, but in particular food or drink, such as issue rum.

jack, a A Military Policeman. There are a dozen possible derivations for this word, but the most likely is an early 18th-century term 'jack in office' meaning a petty official. See also *nit*, *Red Caps*.

Jack Horner	A corner.
Jacko	A Turk, mostly used by Australian troops. See also *Abdul*, *Johnny*.
jag, to be on the	Heavy drinking, believed to be from the Cumbrian term to go on a drinking spree.
jake	Good, mostly Canadian.
jakes	Latrines, a word dating back at least to Elizabethan times.
jam on it, to have	To be fortunate, or to be grateful for what you have. 'I got a double rum ration.' 'Well chum, you've got jam on it.'
jam tart	Heart.
jam tins	A crude hand-grenade made from empty jam tins, packed with gun cotton and scrap metal and ignited by a slow-match fuse. Much used on Gallipoli.
jammy	Lucky, often used as 'jammy bugger'. A shortened variant of *jam on it*.
Jane Shore	A whore.
jankers	A military prison, but more often being confined to quarters.
japan	Bread, being a corruption of the French 'du pain'.
Jenny Lee	Tea.
jerks	Physical training, but to 'put some jerk' into something was to hurry up.
Jerry	German. Post-1916, a term used more than *Fritz* or *Huns*.

Jerry up or Jerry over   A warning that German aircraft were in the vicinity.

jig-a-jig   Sexual intercourse. An English expression that can be traced back to a popular ballad titled 'Jig-a-Jig To The Hirings'. The jig was a dance but the expression became corrupted around the 1840s to mean something more than just dancing. It proved very popular with French civilians during the war.

jigger   An army despatch rider, from the nickname given to motorcycles of the period. The word had many meanings pre-war, the most common being a curse, 'I'll be jiggered', which was a euphemism for 'buggered'. Its use for a motorcycle is probably from its meaning for shaking or jerking something, particularly on French *pavé* roads.

jildi   To hurry up, from a Hindi word. Similar in meaning to *iggry*.

Jimmy or Jimmy Riddle   To urinate, from the rhyming slang 'piddle'.

Joanna   Piano, from the Cockney rhyming slang for 'pianner', meaning joanna.

jock   Any Scottish soldier, or regiment. See also *kiltie*.

Johnny   A Turkish soldier, shortened from Johnny Turk. See also *Abdul*, *Jacko*.

Johnson or Jack Johnson A large, 15cm German artillery shell that burst with a dense black smoke. From the name of the black American boxer, Jack Johnson (1878–1946), world heavyweight champion from 1908–15. See also *Black Maria*, *coal box*, *crump*.

Jolly Polly Gallipoli.

joy-stick The pilot's flight control lever, it originated in the Royal Flying Corps.

jonnock Straightforward, fair. A very popular word during the war, introduced by the Australian troops, but one which had died out by the end of hostilities.

jug Prison or a cell, from early 19th-century American usage, referring to a prison as being like a stone jug. See also *chokey*, *clink*, *cooler*, *coop*, *hutch*.

juice Fuel, originally for an aeroplane, but latterly for any motor vehicle. From the slang for an electrical current.

jump to it To carry out an order or command immediately.

jumping-off trench A trench from which an attack was launched. Sometimes specially constructed for that purpose.

jury, jummage and couter The army knife, fork and spoon. From Hindi.

K1 The first of Lord Kitchener's 100,000 1914 New Army volunteers. Also known as *Kitchener's mob*.

Kamerad

German word for 'comrade'. Not, as often thought, the word for surrender, which was 'übergeben'. However, its frequent use by Germans who wished to be spared gave it a dual meaning.

Kelly's Eye

Number one, used in the game of *House*.

khaki

A drab yellow-fawn colour adopted in 1867 initially for use in the Abyssinian campaign, replacing the hot, impractical and very conspicuous red jackets usually worn. Thereafter it became general issue for all soldiers in colonial campaigns, and it was adopted for European service dress in the army in 1902.

kibosh or kybosh

To spoil, ruin or knock out. First used in print in 1836 by Charles Dickens in 'Boz'.

kiltie

A Highland soldier. See also *jock*.

kip

To sleep, or a place to sleep. In the 19th century it referred to a low-class lodging or doss-house.

kisser

The mouth. Mostly used in threat or jokingly. 'She gave him a right whack across the kisser.'

kit

a slang term from a mid-18th-century definition of the soldier's military equipment. It encompassed every item a soldier possessed, from helmet to boots.

"Combed-out" Gentleman (to pal, also about to be called up).
"What about 'avin' our photos took? We shall be in khaki tomorrow, and I should like to feel I 'ad some record of what I've looked like. (Punch)

Kitchener's blue	The blue uniforms worn by early volunteers as there was insufficient *khaki* available.
Kitchener's mob or men	1914 volunteers. See *K1*.
kite	A pilot's term for his aircraft, from the frail children's toys.
kite balloon	An observation balloon, anchored to the ground by a cable.
Kiwi	A New Zealand soldier.
klaxon	A very loud air-horn. Often used to signal Morse code to the ground by balloon observers.

knapper　　　　　The head.

knapsack　　　　　A large khaki webbing pack carried
on the back, containing spare
clothes, iron rations, ground sheet
etc. See also *valise*.

knife-rest　　　　An X-shaped wooden frame with
barbed wire wound around it. They
were portable and used as trench
barricades or to block gaps in wire
entanglements.

knobkerrie　　　　From the Irish word for *trench club*.

knobs on, with　　The same to you – only more so! A
pre-war children's insult, usually
good humoured.

knock it back　　　To drink.

knock off　　　　An example of an expression with
multiple, and contradictory,
meanings. In its first sense it meant
to cease working, but in the second it
was to complete a job hurriedly, as in
'The colonel knocked off that trench
tour tout sweet.' It could also mean
to steal.

knocking shop　　A brothel, from the 16th-century
word 'knocking', or having sex. See
also *red lamp*.

knuts　　　　　People of some standing or
importance. It was allegedly the
nickname given to senior officers by
the Dover Patrol who often escorted
them to France. It became a
tongue-in-cheek term for anyone

	who regarded themselves as a cut above the rest. See also *heads, toughs*.
KR	Kings Regulations. The military bible of routine, procedures and orders.
lachrymatory shells or gas	A form of tear-gas that irritated the mucous membranes and caused the eyes to water uncontrollably and the affected man to sneeze continually. Unpleasant but rarely fatal.
lance jack	A lance-corporal, the lowest rank of NCO.
landowner	To be killed, or dead and buried. See also *cop it, huffed, pushing up daisies, snuff it*.
last hope	The *iron rations*.
latrine rumour	See *Chinese whispers, cookhouse rumour, furphy*.
laughing	To be comfortable, in a *cushy* job or wounded. 'He copped a Blighty one, and he's laughing.'
lead swinger	A malingerer, someone who wanted to evade his duty. From the naval term 'heaving the lead' to take depth soundings, which soldiers believed to have been a very easy job, which it wasn't.
Leaning Virgin	The golden statue on the roof of the basilica of Notre-Dame de Brebières in Albert. Struck by a German shell in 1915, she canted over at an

extreme angle and was chained in place by Royal Engineers. The rumour grew that when she fell, the war would end. In fact, she was shot down by British artillery in June 1918. See also *Fanny Durack*.

leap frogging
The system of using assault troops to capture and hold an objective, while successive waves of men pass them to move on to the next objective.

Lebel Ma'm'selle
The French Lebel M.1893 service rifle. From the pun 'La belle Mademoiselle'.

leg, show a
leg-show
To get out of bed, a naval expression. A vaudeville act similar to the French Can-Can routine, where girls in stockings and short skirts danced to popular songs. In the days of Victorian innocence, this was considered to be pretty racy stuff. Such acts often drew furious complaints from more sober-minded members of the public, but the soldiers loved it.

Legs Eleven
Number seven in the game of *House*.

Letters up
See *mail up*.

Lewis gun
The .303in Lewis Light machine gun. Invented by an American, Colonel Isaac Lewis, in 1911, it was manufactured under licence

	by BSA in Birmingham. Over 50,000 were produced.
liaison officer	Responsible for informing the various armies, corps or divisions what was happening.
lid	A steel helmet. A term still in use today for a motorcycle helmet. See also *battle bowler*, *pot*, *pudding basin*, *tin hat*.
light duty	Men who were not seriously ill were placed by the medical officer (*MO*) on light duty. This inevitably meant doing heavy manual work; however, many MOs recognized that soldiers needed a break from the punishing trench routine and were often sympathetic, giving a few days 'light' to men they believed would benefit. See also *MD*.
Light Horse	An Australian mounted infantry regiment, highly respected for their fighting qualities.
limber	The two-wheeled portion of a gun carriage that contained the ammunition.
Linseed Lancers	The Royal Army Medical Corps.
lip	Impudence or abuse, a civilian word from the 1820s.
listening post	A concealed advanced position close to the enemy's lines. Also an underground chamber in a mine

working, for the purpose of listening to enemy mining activity.

little grey home in the west A vest or army shirt, from the popular song of the time. Particularly apposite, because the army shirts were the home to hundreds of lice.

Little Willie The German Crown Prince. Also the prototype tank, manufactured in the autumn of 1915.

live one A live fuzed shell. To be handled with care.

lively A classic British understatement to describe heavy shellfire, usually preferred by officers.

loaf o' bread Head.

Lochnagar The vast mine crater at La Boisselle on the Somme. So named from the reserve trench in which the original mineshaft was dug. See also *mine*.

Lone Pine An infamous, hard-fought area on Gallipoli.

lone star A second lieutenant. See also *pip*.

long eared chum A horse or mule. See also *GS hairy*.

long haired chum A girlfriend.

Longhorn The Maurice Farman LS7 biplane. Too slow and frail for combat, it was taken out of service in 1915.

look stick A trench periscope.

look-in at To be offered or shared something, as in 'The cook gave me a look-in at some gash stew.'

loophole

A small aperture in a *parapet* or steal plate through which a soldier could fire or observe the enemy.

loophole plate

A bullet-proof steel plate, approximately 24in x 18in with an oval aperture in it that could be closed by means of a hinged plate. Mostly used by snipers, when properly camouflaged they were undetectable.

loopy or looby

Daft or slightly mad. From the Scots 'loopy' or crafty.

loot

A lieutenant. Not an Americanism, but a British term that originated during the war, as a more specific term, i.e. a 'second loot', or 'one pip loot', defining a subaltern. American troops later adopted it to mean any grade of lieutenant.

Lord Lovell

A shovel.

Lord Mayor

Swear.

lorry jumping or hopping

The art of hitching lifts on passing army lorries to get to one's destination. It often meant being polite to Army Service Corps drivers, possibly the only time an infantryman ever did so.

louse trap

A woollen body belt supposed to attract lice. Also the issue sleeveless sheepskin coats, which certainly achieved the same effect. See also *stinkers*.

lousy with
Crawling with lice, or sometimes Germans.

Lousy Wood
Leuze Wood, Somme. On high ground just above the village of Combles, it proved a costly objective to capture and finally fell on 4–5 September 1916.

lucifer
A popular brand of match. Refer to the song 'Pack Up Your Troubles' (reproduced later in this book).

lumbered, to be
To be found out, or given additional punishment or work. Originally a thieves' word from the early 19th century for being arrested.

Lyddite
A compound of picric acid that was manufactured in Lydd in Kent from 1888 for use in artillery shells.

Macaroni
An Italian soldier.

mace
See *trench club*.

machonochie
Named after its Aberdeen manufacturer, it was a tinned vegetable stew consisting of carrots, potato and turnips which was edible if heated up. As fresh vegetables or fruit were conspicuously lacking from the soldier's diet, it was relatively popular. Unsurprisingly, after the war the company went out of business.

mad minute
Every pre-war regular army soldier was able to shoot 15 aimed rounds per minute.

mafeesh Nothing, all finished, gone. From the same Arabic word, it was sometimes just shortened to maff. Popular on Gallipoli but not so on the Western Front.

magazine The metal box or tube on a rifle for cartridges, or the store for artillery shells. It was also a famous billet in Ypres.

maghnoon Fool, idiot, from the Arabic word.

mail up The shout all soldiers loved. Mail from home was one of the few high points in trench life and helped keep morale up, and the post was rarely delayed.

make To acquire, or steal. From thieves' slang of the 18th century.

male See *tank*.

mandarin A pompous, generally useless senior officer.

map, off the Quite literally not visible either on a map or by eye. Often used to describe some event that defied explanation.

marching order, full What an infantryman carried when marching from one location to another, basically, everything he required to survive. The total weight was often 70–80lb.

mate A friend or comrade but often just a convivial way of greeting a fellow soldier. It is old English and dates back at least to the mid-15th century.

A Maxim Maxim
"Fire should be withheld till a favourable target presents itself."
(Bruce Bairnsfather, author's collection)

	Also used as 'matey'. See also *chum*, *cobber*, *pal*.
matlow	A sailor, from the French word 'matelot'.
maternity jacket	The Royal Flying Corps wore a khaki double-breasted tunic with short collar so no tie was required.
Maxim	The German 7.92mm Model MG08 machine gun, designed by American Hiram Maxim. It was the predominant German medium machine gun of the war.
MC	Military Cross. See Appendix 6.
MD	Medicine and duty. A pill (often the *No. 9*) was given to a man who reported sick and he was then ordered to report to his NCO for *light duty*.
MEF	Mediterranean Expeditionary Force which landed at Gallipoli.
Mespot	Mesopotamia, one of the forgotten theatres of conflict. British forces landed in the Persian Gulf to fight the Turks, and initially suffered heavy defeats. Baghdad was eventually captured but for much of the time ground conditions made fighting impossible.
messcart	A wagon, usually four-wheeled, in which officers' kit and items such as folding chairs and tables and camp beds were carried. In fact, anything that was of use or comfort

	tended to find a place on the company messcarts.
mess-tin	Another name for the *canteen*.
Methuseliers	An Australian re-mount unit comprising of men over-age for front-line duty.
Micks	Any Irish unit.
MiD	Mentioned in Despatches. See Appendix 6.
mike	To evade duty or make oneself scarce. From an early 19th-century civilian expression meaning to lounge about and do nothing.
Military Police	Largely detested and regarded as existing only to make soldiers' lives a misery, they actually performed much vital work, such as directing traffic under heavy shellfire. See also *nit*, *Red Caps*.
Mills grenade	The No. 5 hand grenade, based on an earlier Belgian design but improved and patented by Sir William Mills. Despite popular lore, the segments cast in to the body existed solely to provide grip in wet or muddy conditions and did not aid fragmentation. Over 65 million were manufactured during the war. See also *grenade*.
mince pies	Eyes.
mine	An explosive charge placed underground, designed to blow large

	gaps in the enemy's line. Areas such as Loos and Vimy were notorious for mining. See also *Lochnagar*.
Minnie	A class of German short-range mortars, properly known as the 'Minenwerfer'. Their explosions were devastatingly destructive. See also *flying pig*, *plum pudding*, *Stokes mortar*, *trench mortar*.
MM	Military Medal. See Appendix 6.
MO, the	The medical officer, who worked in the line with an infantry battalion or artillery battery.
mob	An all-encompassing word for a man's battalion, company or platoon. Popular with Australian and New Zealand troops.
money for jam	Sometimes 'money for old rope'. An easy job.
mongey	Food, from the French 'manger', to eat.
mongey wallah	A cook or cook's assistant. From the French 'manger', to eat.
Mons man	One of the original BEF regular soldiers who had been in France since the start of the war. They became increasingly rare. See also *BEF*.
mop it down	To empty a glass, from *c.* 1810.
mopping up	The task of dealing with isolated bodies of enemy troops (often snipers) who had been by-passed by

the initial assault. Sections of men were designated 'mopping up troops'. It was often hard and bloody fighting with little quarter given. An expression probably based on *mop it down*.

Morse code
The simple dot and dash code invented by Samuel Morse (1791– 1872) much used to send telegraphic messages.

Mouquet Farm
A large farm on Pozières ridge. Also known as 'Mucky Farm' and 'Moo-Cow Farm', it was the scene of the bloodiest fighting by the Australians on the Somme, where they lost 23,000 men on the ridge in 43 days.

mouth organ
The *Stokes mortar* bomb, nicknamed such from the wailing noise the shell made.

MSM
Meritorious Service Medal. See Appendix 6.

muck in
To share everything with friends, be it food, sleeping quarters or trench duties.

mucker
A friend. A Cockney word that originally meant to take a heavy fall, but how it transmogrified into 'friend' is a mystery. It was often used by Australian troops.

mud hook
The anchor in the game of *Crown and Anchor*.

mufti   Civilian clothes. The word seems to have appeared in the early 19th century but its origin is unclear.

mulligan   Camp stew. A pre-war Americanism from the name for Irish stew.

mustard gas   Introduced by the Germans in Ypres in September 1917 (and subsequently known as Yperite) it was fired in shells marked with a yellow cross. It was odourless and caused severe burning and blistering. See also *blue cross shell*, *green cross shell*, *yellow cross shell*.

Mutt and Jeff   The War and Victory medals, named after two popular comic characters created by Bud Fisher in 1907. See also *Pip, Squeak and Wilfred*.

nail   To steal, from the mid-18th-century word to catch or secure.

name, to have one's taken   To have one's name and number noted by an NCO for an infringement of military law.

napoo   Empty, finished, no longer existing. A much used word probably taken from the French 'Il n'y en a plus', there's no more.

nark   One who tries to gain favour by informing on others. From an earlier expression for a police informant.

NBG   No bloody good.

NCO   Non-commissioned officer, i.e. a corporal or sergeant.

next of kin Every soldier's *pay book* had to have the address of a relative who could be informed if he were killed or wounded.

nick Either a military jail, or to steal. In the 19th century it was used in the context of arresting a thief, but its earlier use, dating from the 16th century, meant to cheat or defraud.

nicky A carefully preserved cigarette stub kept behind the ear, a wartime word.

night ops A night training operation, usually farcical due to lack of communication.

Nine Two A German '9.2'in shell much feared for its destructive power. In fact the Germans did not use a calibre of this size, and it was most likely the 21cm Heavy Howitzer.

Nissen hut A small half-circular hut of *corrugated iron*, invented in 1916 by Major Peter Nissen, 29th Field Company, Royal Engineers. One could be erected by six men in four hours.

nit A Military Policeman, because they were always in your hair. See also *cherry nob*, *Red Caps*.

nix Nothing, from the German 'nichts'. One of the few trench words used by British, French, American and German soldiers.

Noah's doves The reinforcements that were still

arriving after the Armistice was
signed.

no bon
Not good, from the French. See also
bon.

No. 9
The universal purgative pill for
soldiers on sick duty. A universal
laxative pill, given when no other
remedy was deemed suitable. It
gave rise to the bingo call
'Doctor's orders – number nine.'

Nobby
Anyone named Clark. The most
plausible explanation is that in the
19th century '*nobby*' meant posh, or
smartly attired. Office clerks were
required to be smartly dressed and
were regarded as 'nobs'.

No-Man's Land
The unoccupied area between
opposing front-line trenches varying
between 20 and 600 yards in
width. It was a nightmare
wasteland of rusty wire, rotting
corpses and trench filth and it
became symbolic of the Great
War. The term was actually very
ancient, having been recorded
in an English Government Roll dated
1320 as '*nomannesland*' and it was
used by Daniel Defoe in 'Robinson
Crusoe' to define a border region.

non-stop
A high-flying heavy shell that has
passed overhead. From the sound
made by an express train.

north and south — Mouth.

not half — A pre-war Cockney catchphrase which was soon universally used in the army. It had varied meanings, but was mostly used as an affirmative. 'Are you on leave tomorrow?' 'Not half.'

number on it — A superstition that only a bullet or shell with a man's regimental number on it could hit him.

number up, to have one's — To be in trouble or be convinced one is going to get wounded or killed.

numerals — Also 'titles'. The brass or cloth lettering worn on the shoulder-straps denoting the regiment, i.e. RF for Royal Fusiliers.

nut — See *one of the boys*.

nuts — French slang for bullets. They used several words, chatâignes, pralines, pruneaux, and this was picked up by the British soldiers, who sometimes referred to the German slinging nuts at them.

nut, to do one's — Originally to desert but later in the war it meant to lose one's temper, or go slightly mad.

NYD — Medically, it meant Not Yet Diagnosed. Soldiers said it meant Not Yet Dead.

observer — In the army, a signaller, artilleryman or sniper who used a telescope or binoculars to watch the enemy's trenches. In the airforce, he was occupant of the rear (or sometimes forward) cockpit whose job was to man the machine gun against enemy attack, and to spot enemy activity on the ground.

OC Officer Commanding.

ocean pearl A girl.

Ocean Villas The village of Auchonvillers on the Somme.

odds and sods Soldiers attached to an HQ to be used as messengers, batmen, clerks etc.

odds, to shout the To brag or curse loudly, from the noise made by bookmakers on the racecourse.

off duty Those rare moments when men were not required for any military purpose.

off it To die.

offensive A large-scale attack, such as the Somme Offensive. HQ frequently sent missives to line regiments asking if they were being 'sufficiently offensive'. As a result the word became regarded with cynical humour. A famous cartoon in the *Wipers Times* depicted a young officer musing 'Am I being offensive enough?'

office, the The cockpit of an aircraft.

oh my

A sword. An abbreviated form of rhyming slang, 'Oh my Gawd'.

O I/C

Officer in charge of a small unit such as signallers or snipers, often a subaltern.

oil, the

A truthful statement. Mostly Australian.

oil-can

A large 24cm German *trench mortar* that could throw a 180lb shell 2,500 yards.

old bean

A familiar greeting from popular music hall culture, similar to the French 'mon vieux'. See also *old boy*, *old chap*, *old man*.

Old Bill

Originally the lugubrious cartoon character invented in 1914/15 by Bruce Bairnsfather (1887–1959). Bill was the archetypal BEF soldier, who had been 'out since Mons'. This gave rise to many old sweats being given the nickname.

old boy

See *old bean*.

old chap

See *old bean*.

Old Contemptibles

The original regular army of pre-1914. Allegedly because of a comment from Kaiser Wilhelm, describing the BEF as 'A contemptible little army', although the original expression seems to come from a report about the German Army being able to 'walk over (Sir John) French's contemptibly small army'.

Unappetising
Moments when the Savoy, the Alhambra, and the Piccadilli Grill seems very far away
(the offensive starts in half and hour). (Bruce Bairnsfather, author's collection)

old man

The colonel in charge of a battalion but also a familiarity, usually between officers. See also *skipper*.

old soldier

An experienced man who knew all the tricks for avoiding work and had most probably been a pre-war regular soldier.

old sweat

Much the same as *old soldier*.

on the level

Honest. An Americanism from *c*. 1900 adopted into common usage by about 1910.

on the make

To acquire illegally or by *scrounging*. From 17th-century thieves' slang, 'make' being to steal.

on the mat

In front of the CO for a *dressing down*. See also *dressing down*, *high jump*, *on the peg*.

on the never

To obtain something without payment, from the civilian term. See also *wangle*, *win*.

on the peg

Waiting to be disciplined, i.e. hanging around like a coat or hat.

one of the boys or lads

A popular member of a platoon or squad.

ooja or oojah

From 'ooja-cum-pivvy'. A made-up word for a thing or place that the speaker can't remember, similar to a wotsit or *thingummyjig*.

o. pip

observation post.

orchestra

Testicles, from rhyming slang for 'orchestra stalls', meaning 'balls'.

orderly
The soldier accompanying an officer on a tour of inspection.

orderly men
Two men were taken from every platoon daily to act as trench cleaners, ration carriers and general factotums.

orderly officer
The (usually junior) officer selected each day to visit the platoons, check trench stores, cleanliness etc.

orderly room
The office (more often *dug-out*) that was the administrative centre for the battalion.

orderly sergeant or corporal
His duties were similar to that of the *orderly officer*.

orders
The list of crimes and punishments pinned up daily outside the *orderly room*.

OTC
Officer Training Corps.

other ranks (O/Rs)
NCOs and privates.

outfit
Any military unit, mainly Australian.

over the bags or
The beginning of an attack by

over the top
literally climbing over the sand-bag *parapet* to form up and head across No-Man's Land. Its use as an expression to define something that was impossible or excessive did not become commonplace until the late 20th century.

pack
An infantryman's kit, carried by means of webbing or leather straps comprising ammunition pouches, water bottle, *haversack*

and *knapsack* with bayonet, clothing, rations, etc. Additionally most men had to carry extra items, such as bags of *grenades*, ammunition, picks, shovels and rations. Officers did not normally carry packs.

pack-drill
Drill in full marching order undertaken at high speed given as a fairly severe punishment.

pack-horse
A horse or mule used for carrying supplies up to the front line. The armies were largely horse-drawn still, and these animals were invaluable. Over 58,000 died in the war.

packet, to cop a
To be wounded fatally or slightly. See also *cop it*.

pack up
To stop working, retire or otherwise cease functioning. 'The engine's packed up.'

padre
The army chaplain. These varied from the highly respected, who shared trench life with their men and were always a source of cigarettes and comfort, to the despised, who preached loudly about duty but were never seen in the line.

pahny or panny
Water, from a Hindi word.

pakaru
A Maori term for destroyed, broken or unserviceable, mostly used by New Zealand troops.

pal	A friend or comrade. In its original 18th-century form, it meant a thieves' accomplice and was from the Romany word 'palal' or 'palla', a friend. See also *chum, cobber, mate*.
parachute flare	A rocket-fired flare suspended from a small parachute that took a long time to land.
parados	The rearward side of a trench facing away from the enemy. From a French term.
parapet	The forward side of the trench facing the enemy, normally topped with protective sandbags. Like *parados*, derived from a French term.
park	An artillery or tank enclosure.
Paris Gun	A long-barrelled (69ft) fixed gun of around 20cm calibre, used by the Germans to shell Paris between August and November 1918. It was the first artillery piece to launch a shell into the stratosphere, reaching a height of 25 miles.
pass	A highly valued form signed by the *orderly officer* giving the holder permission to travel or be away from his barracks or the line for a specified period.
patrol	The patrolling of No-Man's Land, which took considerable nerve.

patter   The story told by *Crown and Anchor*
                              men. An 18th-century word
                              meaning to talk quickly and glibly.

pavé   The hard cobblestones that French
                              roads were paved with, awful to
                              march on and bone-shaking in a
                              vehicle.

paw   Hand. Mostly used by officers.

pay book   The field service book carried by
                              every soldier that was his personal
                              identification. It contained
                              details of courses attended, pay
                              received and *next of kin*.

PBI   Poor Bloody Infantry. Possibly
                              originating in the *Wipers Times*, it
                              was more commonly used post-1917
                              and much afterwards.

pedlar   Any man named Palmer.
                              Traditionally, a palmer was a robber
                              or trickster, and the word
                              transferred in the 19th century to
                              the trade of peddling, or street
                              selling.

peg, on the   Similar to *on the mat*. In this case it
                              alludes to an item being hung out to
                              dry.

pen and ink   Stink.

perfies   Rumours, predominantly an
                              Australianism. See also *furphy*.

PH helmet   The Phenate Helmet, a gas mask
                              introduced in July 1915 comprising a
                              flannel bag soaked in chemical, with

	two plastic-covered eye holes and a rubber exhalation tube. Crude but the best then available.
phonetic alphabet	Used by signallers. See Appendix 1 for the full alphabet.
phosgene	A choking or pulmonary gas responsible for the majority of gas deaths on the Western Front.
Pickelhaube	The spiked leather German helmet, a much prized souvenir. Not worn in the front lines much after early 1916.
picket	A picket was also an advance guard, stationed close to the enemy line to give warning of any incursions.
piece	A single girl, sexually experienced but not necessarily a prostitute. An early word, dating back at least to the 14th century.
piggy-stick	The wooden shaft of the entrenching tool, carried on straps next to the bayonet. Taken from the children's game 'tip-cat' when a piece of wood thrown into the air was hit by a stick. It made a handy *trench club*.
pig's ear	Beer.
pill-box	A concrete fortification mostly used for machine guns, invented by the Germans. So called due to its resemblance to the medicinal pill box.
pin	A bayonet.
pinch	To steal, from *c.* 1650, and probably from the use by pickpockets (dippers)

to pinch together in their fingers something that was then pocketed. See also *half-inch*, *scrounge*, *snaffle*, *win*.

pineapple grenade	Not really a grenade, but a German M.1916 spigot mortar that fired a finned segmented bomb out to 300 yards.

pioneers	Often, though not exclusively, men who were of over service age or had been wounded, used as labour in and near the front lines. In extremis, they could also be used as fighting troops.

pip	The star worn on the sleeve (after 1916 the shoulder) by a second lieutenant. A lieutenant had two, a captain three.

Pip Emma	Signallers term for pm.

pip-squeak	A small high-velocity artillery shell or sometimes a gas shell. See also *whizz-bang*.

Pip, Squeak and Wilfred	The 1914/15 Star, War and Victory medals. Named after three cartoon characters, a dog, penguin and rabbit, conceived in 1919 by Bertram Lamb.

pipe, put that in your	To make what you will of a fact or event. Its origin is unknown, but it was an expression first used in print by Charles Dickens in 'Pickwick' in 1824.

pipped

Wounded, usually in reference to being hit by a bullet, but sometimes any form of light wound.

pissed

Drunk. A late 19th-century military expression, probably from the need to constantly urinate after drinking too much beer. See also *binge, blanked, blind, blotto, squiffy, tight, zig-zag.*

plank road

Also *corduroy road* and 'wooden track', a timber roadway, laid across flooded or boggy ground designed to carry the weight of wagons or vehicles.

plaster

To shell heavily.

plates of meat

Feet.

platoon

A platoon was theoretically led by a lieutenant, although a corporal or sergeant was more normal. From the French word of the 17th century 'peloton', meaning a small group of soldiers. See Appendix 2.

plink plonk

A corruption of 'vin blanc'. The word 'plonk' is still very much in vogue. See also *point blank.*

plug

To shoot. Originally in the 18th century to 'plug someone' meant to punch them.

Plugstreet

Ploegstreet Wood in Belgium.

plum and apple

A widely issued flavour of jam; in fact at times it seemed to be the only type of jam produced and soldiers longed for other flavours. It spawned a wealth of songs and poems. Demand for it after the war slumped to the point at which it has never since been offered for sale. See also *Tickler's*.

plum duff In normal cookery, a form of plum pudding or suet dumpling, but in the trenches it was made using what was to hand. Crushed hard-tack biscuits, currants, sugar and, if available, a little flour or suet, wrapped in a piece of cloth and boiled, produced a tolerable pudding.

plum pudding The British 2in medium *trench mortar*. The bomb was spherical and fitted to a cast iron shaft. It weighed 60lb but was largely ineffective due to lack of stabilizing and a poor detonating system. Also called the *toffee apple*.

Poilu A 14th-century Italian word for 'young soldier' and used of the French soldiers as *Tommy* was by the British. It actually meant 'hairy', from the fact that most French soldiers were bearded in the early days of the war. The French generally preferred to call themselves 'fantassins' or 'les bonhommes'.

point blank A corruption of 'vin blanc'.

pomfritz The popular dish of fried potatoes, 'pommes frites'.

Pontius Pilate A provost sergeant.

pontoon A bridge of metal cylinders built over a waterway. Later on, any form of temporary bridge.

pony and trap Crap. Going for a 'pony' was to head for the latrines.

poop off A big artillery piece firing.

Pop Poperinghe in Belgium, famous for being the home of *Toc H*.

pork and beans Either the Portuguese infantry or the tinned ration version that consisted mostly of fat and beans, but very little pork.

posh Smart, stylish, well-turned out. Used originally as 'push' or 'poosh', it first appeared in a book by P.G. Wodehouse in 1903.

posh up To smarten up.

possy A military position. Mostly used by Australians. Not to be confused with *pozzie*.

pot Steel helmet. Also known as *battle bowler*, *lid*, *pudding basin*, *steel jug*, *tin hat*.

potato digger The Colt machine gun, from the angled operating arm that moved to and fro underneath as it fired.

potato masher The German Model 24 Stielhandgranate so-called because its long wooden handle resembled

	the civilian potato masher. Also known as *stick bomb*.
Pozzie or Pozzy	Pozières on the Somme.
pozzy jam	Thought to have originated in South Africa where it was used to define any sweetmeat or preserves but, oddly, brought over by Australian troops and widely adopted across the front.
pozzy wallah	A man addicted to jam.
promenade	A stroll. A question asked by soldiers who wished to take a walk with a French girl, and usually turned down with much laughter.
propaganda	The use of half-truths or even outright lies by governments to influence public thinking. By the end of the war it was almost an art form.
proper	Admirable or excellent.
provost sergeant or provo	The NCO responsible for the care of regimental prisoners. A form of unit policeman.
PT	Physical training.
pudding basin	Steel helmet. Also known as *battle bowler*, *lid*, *pot*, *steel jug*, *tin hat*.
puggled or poggled	Mad, from the Hindi 'pagal'.
pukka	Real, genuine. From the Hindi 'pakkha'.
pull out	The act of harnessing horses to gun *limbers* to remove field artillery from their positions. Later, used as a more general term for the planned withdrawal of any military unit.

pull-through

A strong cord with a cylindrical brass weight at one end loops at the other into which oiled *four by two* cleaning patches were placed. It was then pulled through the rifle barrel to clean it.

pulpit

The confined space of an observation post.

pump ship

Sailors' slang for urinating.

PUO

Pyrexia of unknown origin; an undiagnosed fever. See also *trench fever*.

pup

A Sopwith Pup, a successful single-seater biplane introduced in October 1916 and the first aircraft to be carrier landed.

purge

To grumble about a senior, usually an officer.

push

An attack, usually a big one. The Somme battle was generally referred to as 'The Big Push'. See also *Great or Big Push, show*.

pusher

A biplane with a rear-facing engine mounted behind the pilot. See also *tractor*.

pushing up daisies

Dead. From an expression 'pushing up the daisies with his toes'. First recorded in print in 1837. See also *landowner*.

put it across

To take advantage of, or sometimes to physically hit.

put up

To be paraded in front of the CO.

put wise

To be informed, a late war expression brought over by the US troops and widely adopted.

puttee

A cloth band that was wrapped around the leg from ankle to below the knee and the bane of a soldier's life. It was designed to give support when walking, but in the wet trench conditions it restricted blood flow to the feet and led to *trench foot*.

putty medal

One that was earned too easily or was regarded as worthless.

Quakers

A religious group that did not believe in fighting. Many were subjected to harsh treatment from the authorities and some joined the army as *stretcher bearers*. See also *conscientious objectors*.

quarter bloke, the

The quartermaster, either an officer of retirement age unsuited to front-line service, or a sergeant. They were responsible for issuing everything a soldier needed, from boots to biscuits, and they had almost unlimited scope for perfidy.

Quarters' English

The peculiar army language used to describe issue clothing or equipment, i.e. a soft cap was 'cap, woollen, peaked, soldier, for the use of'.

queer   Unwell, sick. An Australian word.

quick dick   A fast-firing 60-pdr gun that could launch a shell every 12 seconds.

quiff   Much adopted by *knuts* and *cards*. It was carefully brushed back hair that rose to a peak on the top of the head. Probably from the medieval head-dress called a 'coif'.

race card   A droll term for the Sick Report issued by an *MO*.

RAF   Royal Air Force. Formed by royal warrant on 1 April 1918, it remains the oldest independent air force in the world. See also *RFC*, *RNAS*.

rag   Its 19th century meaning was to question with enthusiasm (as in a debate) or to create a disturbance. By 1900 it had become a public schools term for rough horseplay, or deliberate destruction of property. It was used more by officers than other ranks, as in, 'That five-nine didn't half rag the OP post.'

rag fair   When an NCO or officer inspected the entire equipment of individual soldiers and missing items had to be paid for.

ragtime   A very popular form of music in syncopated time that post-war evolved into jazz. The word became used to describe anyone or anything that was believed to be absurd or ineffectual, such as Fred Karno's ragtime infantry.

RAMC

Royal Army Medical Corps. Officers and men who were responsible for the collection and treatment of wounded. The cynical referred to them as Rob All My Comrades, as personal items of the wounded often went missing in transit. In reality the RAMC men worked tirelessly and often gallantly under appalling conditions and thousands of men owed their lives to their care. Sometimes also known as 'Rats After Mouldy Cheese'.

Ramparts, the

The wall surrounding the town of Ypres.

rapid fire

To aim and shoot a rifle as fast as possible.

raspberry, to blow a

To make a fart-like noise, usually by blowing through a closed fist. From the rhyming slang for 'raspberry tart', a fart.

rat and mouse

A house.

ration dump

A stockpile of military supplies, ammunition, food etc, near to the front line.

ration party

Men detailed to collect rations from a brigade or divisional store, to be delivered to the front lines. Sometimes called a *carrying party*.

rations
Usually of two types. Wet Rations were cooked food, for example porridge, stew, hot tea, while dry rations included cheese, butter, jam, loose tea.

RAVC
Royal Army Veterinary Corps.

razzle, to be on the
Originally to have riotous fun. An abbreviated form of 'razzle-dazzle' which was a form of rapidly circulating fairground ride popular pre-war. The wobbly sensation experienced afterwards was similar to being tipsy. By 1914 the meaning had changed somewhat and it meant more of a drunken binge than simply having fun.

RE
Royal Engineers. Responsible for all military construction work.

reconnoitre
Its literal meaning was to go in search of enemy positions but it became a euphemism used when a soldier was on the *scrounge*.

Red Baron
Manfred Albrecht Freiherr von Richthofen (2 May 1892–21 April 1918). Probably the best-known fighter pilot of the war, with 80 kills falling to his guns. He was shot down and killed, probably by an Australian machine-gunner named Sergeant Cedric Popkin of the 24th Machine Gun Company. See also *Flying Circus*.

Red Caps
Military Police, so called because of the red cover worn over their soft caps. Men volunteered for the post, and it was believed that few decent soldiers would do it. See also *battle police*, *cherry nob*, *nit*.

Red Cross
An impartial humanitarian society formed in Switzerland in 1870 whose members worked during the war in refugee centres and hospitals and as ambulance drivers and whose clerical staff recorded the names of the wounded, missing and dead.

red lamp
A licensed brothel, from the lamp hung outside. See also *knocking shop*.

red tabs
Staff officers, from the red collar patches worn on their uniforms. They were much despised by line infantrymen. See also *staff*.

redoubt
A very strongly fortified position in a front-line trench, usually very heavily protected by barbed wire, containing machine guns. Two very infamous examples were the Hohenzollern and Schwaben redoubts.

refilling point
A divisional dump where petrol, water or other liquids were supplied.

regiment
A unit of the army that contained several battalions. The source of

much pride among those that served within it. See Appendix 2.

Regimental, the
The regimental sergeant major, one for each battalion, usually a strict disciplinarian.

regimental police
Men appointed from a regiment's ranks to act as guards and escort. Not *Red Caps*.

registering
The method by which artillery determined the range of enemy targets, usually by firing carefully observed rounds and making corrections. Too much fire could alarm an enemy unit and force them to move. See also *bracketing*.

relief
When one man or unit replaces another in the line. An old expression, used in Shakespeare's 'Hamlet', 'For this relief, much thanks'.

reserve trench
The third in the line of trenches facing the enemy, from which, as its name suggests, reserve troops could be brought forwards. See also *support trench*.

reserved occupation
Men whose jobs were considered vital to the war effort, and were excluded from military service.

respirator
The Small Box Respirator, introduced in early 1917, comprising a close-fitting rubber mask with eye pieces and a rubber hose connecting

to a metal filtration unit. They were effective against all gases except *mustard gas*.

rest camp Tented or wooden camps behind the line where soldiers coming down from the line would be housed.

THE OLD FORMULA.

Wife. "Look, George – my new respirator."
George (preoccupied). "Oh! By Jove – yes! Suits you devilish well, my dear. (Punch)

	Usually there was little rest to be had there. Occasionally used as a term for a cemetery.
Reveille	The wake-up bugle call. Usually accompanied by the shout 'rise and shine'. Followed by loud cursing from the recumbent soldiers.
revet	A medieval term for facing an embankment or trench with stone. By 1914–18 it meant to reinforce trench walls with timber or metal posts to strengthen them, often with chicken wire or *corrugated iron* to add support.
RFA	Royal Field Artillery characterized by their light field guns, pulled by horses.
RFC	Royal Flying Corps. Formed in April 1912, it remained an independent service until merged with the Royal Naval Air Service in April 1918 to become the Royal Air Force. See also *RAF*.
rhyming slang	Originating in the East End of London, it was thought to have been started by costermongers and street sellers in the 1840s, although whether it was invented deliberately or accidentally is undetermined. Throughout the war it remained predominantly the preserve of soldiers of the London regiments.

Richard	Faeces, from the rhyming slang for 'Richard the Third', meaning 'turd'. The brown-white observation balloons were also so named, possibly because of their resemblance to one.
ricko	A bullet ricochet.
righto	An affirmative, popular with officers.
River Ouse	Booze.
RNAS	The Royal Naval Air Service. Formed in 1912, it was the flying branch of the Royal Navy. In April 1918 it was merged with the Royal Flying Corps to form the Royal Air Force. See also *RAF*.
RND	Royal Naval Division, a unit formed in 1914 from naval and marine volunteers and reservists who couldn't be employed at sea. They were used as infantry but retained their naval ranks.
Robin Hood	No good.
rock and boulder	Shoulder.
rocker, off one's	Mad, unhinged.
roll call	Usually first thing in the morning, men would have their names called out to be accounted for, and when completed, the platoon sergeant would state 'All present and correct sir.' This was often done after an attack, to determine who had survived.

roll on demob
A nickname for the Railway Operating Department engines, marked ROD. Also often used by weary men who wanted to leave the army, preferably immediately.

Roody Boys
Rue du Bois, near Neuve Chapelle.

rooky or rookie
A corruption of the word recruit.

rooty
Bread, from the Urdu word 'roti'.

rooty medal
The regular army long service medal. Its award was often described as '18 years of undetected crime'.

Rosalie
The French soldiers' nickname for their epée bayonet.

rosebuds
Potatoes, i.e. spuds.

Ross rifle
The Canadian Model 1910 .303in Ross, a finely made rifle that did not function well in muddy trench conditions or with poor-quality ammunition. Replaced by the Lee Enfield in 1916.

Rosy Lee
Tea.

rough house
Originally a late 19th-century American expression for disorder or a quarrel. By the turn of the century it had come to mean a fight, usually fuelled by drink.

round the houses
Trousers. It was pronounced 'round the ha'ses' to rhyme with the Cockney pronunciation 'trahsers'.

route, column of
An infantry column four abreast for marching. Officers marched at the front, NCOs in spaces in between.

route march

Marching over a pre-planned route as part of physical training. Sometimes this could cover 20 miles and it was a harsh test of physical endurance, hated by most but necessary to ensure the required level of fitness.

RTO

The Railway Transport Officer. An officer whose job was to ensure that men could get to the ports for leave, or rejoin their regiments in the line. He was also responsible for the evacuation of wounded. Most of the time they had less idea of where line regiments were than the soldiers themselves. An unenviable job, but efficient RTOs were worth their weight in gold.

rum jar

A German 24.5cm Erhardt Ladungswerfer *trench mortar*, so called because of its similarity to the stoneware British rum jar. See also *SRD*.

run, on the

To have the enemy retreating, from the criminal expression for trying to evade the police.

runner

A soldier whose job was to transport messages from company HQ to battalion or brigade HQ. In essence, little different to the methods employed by the Ancient Greeks or Romans. It was thankless and

	dangerous, and not for nothing were runners the most decorated group of private soldiers.
rush	To cheat or overcharge. Pre-war street cant, as in 'How much did they rush you for that beer?'
Russian sap	A *sap* that normally did not break the surface of the ground, so it could remain concealed from the enemy.
Russki	A Russian soldier. A brigade of Russians did fight on the Western Front but mutinied after the 1917 revolution.
SAA	Small arms ammunition.
Salonika	Like Mesopotamia, a forgotten battle front where British troops were sent to aid the Serbs to fight Bulgaria. Most casualties were from disease rather than combat.
san fairy ann	It doesn't matter, it's not important, don't worry about it. From the French 'ça ne fait rien', it doesn't matter.
sandbag	A hessian or burlap sack of roughly 14in x 26in, filled with earth as protection against bullets, splinters and other missiles. Soldiers spend an inordinate amount of time filling them.
sanitary duty	The least popular fatigue in the army, filling old latrine trenches with *chloride of lime*, digging new ones as

well as emptying the latrine buckets. Strangely, some men actually enjoyed the duty as it kept them away from the more dangerous fatigues. See also *turd walloper*.

sankey A 5-franc note, from the French 'cinq', five.

sap A trench made by digging outwards from an existing front line one, usually into No-Man's Land. See also *Russian sap*.

sapper A Royal Engineer, from their ancient art of trench excavation. The term has been suggested to date back as far as the Assyrians.

sarn't An abbreviation of sergeant, as is 'sgt'. During the war, it was spelled in the traditional manner 'Serjeant' and this changed to 'Sargeant' only in 1953, although the Rifles still retain the old spelling.

sausage A squat German observation balloon.

Sausage Eaters The Germans.

sawmill An army operating theatre.

scatty Slightly mad or eccentric. Possibly derived from 'scatter-brained'.

Schwartzbrot Black rye bread given to British prisoners of war. Similar in taste to sawdust.

scoff To eat, or food generally from the Afrikaans 'skoff', meaning food. It was brought back to Britain by sailors

	around 1850 and widely adopted. See also *scran*.
Scotch pegs	Legs.
scran	Food generally, or to provide a meal. A word that dates at least from the mid-18th century. 'On the scran' meant begging for scraps.
screw picket	A long (5ft or longer) corkscrew-shaped stake made from sprung steel that was screwed into the ground and then draped with barbed wire. Almost indestructible.
scrim	*Camouflage* netting.
scrounge	To steal from official sources or other units, but never from one's mates. Scrounging could cover anything, firewood, food or items of lost kit. It originated from a West Country dialectic word 'scrunge' meaning to steal fruit off trees. An efficient scrounger was much prized in every platoon.
scuppered	A naval expression for dead, referring to the sinking of a vessel. Sometimes used to describe a plan or event that failed.
section	A 1914 section comprised 16 men under command of a lance-corporal. Later in the war this reduced to eight men. See Appendix 2.
sector	A military area, defined by that part of the front line and the area behind

it that was held by a company or battalion.

semaphore
Use of flags or arms held at different angles to send a message. Only useful if the enemy weren't within range.

separate peace
Soldiers who were fed-up with the war would suggest that they and their chums made a separate peace with Germany.

sergeant major's
Particularly good tea, usually very strong and sweet.

seven
Regular soldiers enlisted for seven years, and many were released from the army during the early part of the war having 'done their seven'.

Sexton Blake
The provost sergeant, from the popular pre-war detective books.

shave
A rumour, normally from the company barber, who was a fount of all knowledge.

sheet
A charge sheet for misdemeanours; a man up for punishment was often referred to as 'on the sheet'.

shell dressing
Every soldier carried one sewn into his tunic. See also *field dressing*.

shell shock
An acute nervous reaction believed to be due to persistent exposure to shellfire. Only officially recognized in 1916. Symptoms included dizziness, amnesia, uncontrollable shaking, headaches and an inability to speak. In fact it was an extreme reaction to

	stress and could affect men who were not even in the front line. Rest helped but some severe cases never recovered.
shell splinters	Usually incorrectly referred to as *shrapnel*, these were lethal fragments of high-explosive shell casing ranging in size from a fingernail to 2ft long or more. They were thick, razor-edged and capable of cutting a man in two or inflicting the most appalling wounds.
shelter	A word used in its broadest sense by soldiers to denote any form of protection from the weather or enemy activity, although technically it refers to a properly constructed *dug-out*. See *dug-out*, *funk hole*.
shirty	Cross, angry or argumentative, from London street slang of the mid-19th century.
shit or shite	Originally a medieval word for excrement, probably from the German word 'Scheisse'. During the First World War it was often used as a generic term for the pervading mud. A man of bad character was sometimes referred to as a shit. See *four letter man*.
shock troops	Originating in the German Army as 'Sturmtruppen' or storm-troops, they were fast moving, heavily

armed troops whose job was to quickly overrun and pass through enemy defences.

short arm inspection   Undertaken by the *MO* to detect venereal disease. Never done in private, it was a humiliating ordeal for most soldiers.

short hairs   To have a man by the short hairs was to have him a position of disadvantage. From the short hairs on the back of the neck, which were very painful if pulled.

shot up the back   To be put out of action, either physically or mechanically. Originally a Royal Flying Corps expression.

show   A military attack but also a popular theatrical event for soldiers out of the line. See also *push*, *stunt*.

shrapnel   An artillery shell containing lead or steel balls, which exploded in mid-air. Invented in 1784 by Lieutenant Henry Shrapnel (1761–1842) of the Royal Artillery as 'spherical case shot'. Not to be confused with *shell splinters*.

sick parade   When a soldier who was unwell paraded to see the *MO*. He was officially marked in the battalion records as 'Reported sick'.

side kick   A friend or *chum*, predominantly Canadian.

signalese   The use of the signallers' alphabet. See Appendix 1.

Silent Percy

A large-calibre artillery piece that shelled Ypres on a regular basis. The shells exploded with no warning of their approach.

SIW

A self-inflicted wound. If proven it was regarded as a serious crime but some medical officers, aware of the stresses men were under, were prepared to cover it up.

six by four

Army toilet paper.

skilly

A thin watery stew, commonly served in workhouses pre-war.

skin

Next of kin.

skint

Broke, or having lost one's money. From 'skinned', i.e. having had one's skin removed.

skipper

Officers' slang for a company commanding officer.

skirt

Any young woman, dating back at least to the 16th century.

skite

To boast or try to impress. An Australian word.

skive

To evade work. Its origin is unclear but it may be from a Lincolnshire word for lazy.

skrimshanker

A malingerer or work-shy man.

sky-pilot

The *padre*. A naval term from the mid-19th century, referring to the transferring of souls up to heaven.

slacks

An officers' term for trousers worn without puttees.

SM, the

The sergeant major.

smellie

The .303 calibre, Short Magazine Lee Enfield Rifle, standard issue to all British and Imperial troops. The 'short' referred to the barrel length, not the magazine capacity.

smoke

A cigarette. See also *fag*, *gasper*, *nicky*. Other names for cigarettes included *brads*, *coffin nails*, *dags*.

smoke, the

London, a descriptive 19th-century street word.

Smudger

See *Darky*.

smutty

Dirty or obscene.

snaffle

To steal, from the 18th-century word for a horse thief, a 'snaffler'. See also *half-inch*, *pinch*, *scrounge*, *win*.

snip

The regimental tailor.

snipers

The scourge of the front line. Highly trained riflemen able to pick off a fleeting target, on average within three seconds. Introduced by the German Army in 1914, every army was fielding sniper sections by the end of the war.

sniperscope

A wooden framework attached to a rifle enabling it to be fired over a *parapet* by using a mirror and lanyard, without the soldier exposing himself. Useful only at moderately short ranges.

snob

An army cobbler, the word dating back at least to the late 18th century defining any shoemaker.

snuff it	To die, but not necessarily be killed. From the act of snuffing out a candle.
so long	Goodbye or 'au revoir'. An American expression much used by British officers.
soap and water	Daughter.
sock, to put in it	To shut up, as in 'put a sock in your mouth'.
soft number	A pleasant, undemanding job. Latterly used as 'soft option'.
soft touch	Someone who was easy to persuade to one's own way of thinking. 'Ask for some extra rum, the sergeant's a soft touch.'
soldier's friend	A pink tablet of brass polish, that had to be used wet and so was spat upon. Hence the expression *spit and polish*.
some hopes	An event that was highly unlikely. 'You've put in for leave? Some hopes.'
something to hang things on	An accurate self-description of the ordinary infantryman.
somewhere in France	A journalist's expression for an undefined area of the front line. Often used by soldiers when writing home.
Sopwith Pup	A single-seater biplane introduced in autumn 1916. See also *pup*.
SOS	The marine Morse code distress call 'Save Our Souls' used only if a unit was about to be overrun. It was a call either by telegraph or by

pre-arranged rocket signal for a heavy artillery barrage to aid the defenders. See also *Very light*.

souvenir The French word for a keepsake. Soldiers loved them and all manner of items were collected, from helmets and weapons to embroidered postcards and shell fuzes. It also meant the same as *scrounge*.

spare part A useless soldier.

sparks, getting the Estimating range was often difficult so riflemen and machine gunners would fire into the dense belts of barbed wire to observe bullet strikes from the resultant sparks. Once determined, the exact range would be noted down for future use.

specialists Machine-gunners, signallers, snipers – any soldier who had specific trade training. They were usually paid more than line infantrymen.

spent bullet One that has reached the end of its flight. A hit from one could still cause bad bruising. Occasionally used of a useless soldier.

spit and polish To clean things ready for an inspection, often at battalion level. See also *soldier's friend*.

split arsing An Royal Flying Corps term for low stunt flying, dangerous and often fatal.

spokey A wheelwright.

spout, one up the	To have a loaded round ready in the chamber of a rifle or machine gun.
spud	The nickname for anyone called Murphy, from the generally believed fact that all Irishmen ate nothing but potatoes. Also, post-1916, a large steel plate bolted to the track of a tank to give it better grip.
squad	A small number of soldiers assembled for duty and led by an NCO. See Appendix 2.
square, to	To arrange for something to be done. 'Can you square my sentry duty to be changed with the sergeant?' Sometimes involving a modest bribe. From the army requirement to leave bedding and kit neatly squared on a bed during an inspection.
Squarehead	A German. See also *Boche*, *Fritz*, *Hun*, *Jerry*.
square-pusher	An eligible woman, from the pre-war tradition of soldiers escorting nursemaids around local squares and parks. To go 'square-pushing' meant to dress smartly in the hope of finding a female to accompany.
squiffy	Drunk. Probably from 'skew-whiff', lopsided. See also *binge*, *blanked*, *blind*, *blotto*, *pissed*, *tight*, *zig-zag*.
SRD	The subject of much dispute over the years, it is often stated to mean 'Service Rum Diluted'. Some years

ago several of the one-gallon pottery rum jars were unearthed near Ypres with their original wax seals, which were marked Supply Reserve Depot. The rum was Pusser's single-malt navy rum produced in the British Virgin Isles. It was about 95 per cent proof and would make men cough and their eyes water when the tot of 1/64th gallon was issued at *stand to* every morning. Other names attributed to the initials were 'Sergeants' Rum Distribution', 'Seldom Reaches Destination' and 'Soon Runs Dry' amongst many others.

staff	Either the staff sergeant, or a generic term for any staff officers.
staff crawl	A tour of the trenches by staff officers.
stand at ease	Cheese.
stand to	The times at dusk and dawn when men manned the *parapet* and were extra vigilant in case of attack. When finished, the order 'Stand down' was given.
steady on	To be cautious, or moderate. Predominantly an officer's expression that was very typically English.
stealth raid	A small trench raid, undertaken with no artillery or other form of covering fire.

steel jug

Steel helmet. Also known as *battle bowler*, *lid*, *pot*, *pudding basin*, *tin hat*.

stellenbosched, to be

To be returned home in disgrace, usually only applied to senior officers. Taken from the name of the camp in South Africa to which incompetent officers were sent during the Boer War.

stick grenade or bomb

The German Model 24 'Stielhandgranate' introduced in 1915. Identifiable by its long wooden handle and tin-shaped body. See also *potato masher*.

stick it

To endure and keep going, it was often said to badly wounded men. In September 1914 'Stick it, Welch' were the last words of mortally wounded Captain Mark Haggard and the phrase has become part of the Welch Regiment's military folklore.

stiff, a

A corpse. Also used to describe someone who was clumsy or stupid.

sting the quarter

To persuade the quartermaster that one needed a new item of clothing, no mean feat.

stinkers

The issue goatskin waistcoats, which became noxious when wet.

Stokes gun or mortar

Invented by Mr (later Sir) F.W. Scott-Stokes (1860–1927) in 1915. It was a 3.2in tube-launched mortar that became the basis for the current

family of infantry mortars. It could
send its 11lb shell up to 800 yards
with considerable accuracy. See also
mouth organ.

stonkered or stonked Worn out. From the Italian 'stanco',
exhausted.

stop To be hit by a bullet or shrapnel ball.
'Harry's just stopped one.'

storm troops See *shock troops*.

stout fellow Mostly officers' slang, meaning a
man who was a good chap, reliable or
brave.

strafe A word of several meanings. Adopted
by the British from the German term
meaning to shell heavily, it was
adopted by the airforce to describe
the action of attacking ground targets
by using machine guns. The ferocity
of such attacks was reflected in its
other meaning, to be given a severe
verbal dressing-down by an officer
or NCO. It could also be used
dismissively, as in 'That officer is
useless, strafe him.'

stray bullet Bullet fired at random.

stretcher bearers Men who carried casualties out of the
firing lines to receive medical
attention. It was back-breaking work
and in heavy mud up to six men were
required to work in relays to carry
one stretcher case. Also known as
body snatchers and *undertakers*.

strike me dead	The head.
stripes	See *chevron*.
stripped	Literally stripped of markings of rank and reduced in seniority.
stuck in, to get	To work hard on a physical project, usually trench construction. It seems to date purely from the First World War.
stuff	Heavy shell or sometimes machine-gun fire. 'They're putting some stuff on B company tonight.'
stunt	See *push*, *show*.
sub	A subaltern, first or second lieutenant.
Suicide Club	The Machine Gun Corps, but sometimes also the company snipers.
Suicide Corner	A very dangerous junction where the Dixmude Road entered Ypres.
suicide squad	Often used for any unit that had a particularly dangerous job, but particularly company grenade men, machine gunners, snipers and men picked for *trench raids*.
sump	A pit dug below the *duckboards* in a trench to aid drainage.
sunken road	Commonplace on the Somme, where the road surface was several feet below that of the surrounding fields.
support trench	The second in the line of trenches facing the enemy, to provide support to the men manning the front-line trench. See also *reserve trench*.

swaddy
A private soldier, from the early 18th-century word 'swadkin', a newly enlisted soldier. It has since been adopted as 'squaddy'.

swagger stick
A short cane with a metal head, often bearing the regimental badge. Carried by all ranks when leaving camp in walking-out dress. Many officers led attacks carrying their swagger sticks in one hand and revolver in the other.

swanking
Showy or boastful behaviour, but sometimes applied to a man who lied or told tall stories.

sweating on
Having the expectation of something good happening, like the arrival of a parcel or leave.

sweetheart brooch
A small brooch either made from battlefield debris or professionally produced, usually with a regimental insignia on it. Very popular presents to send home, and available in huge numbers from the towns along the front. See also *trench ring*.

swig
To drink, from the 16th-century word 'swyg'.

swinging the lead
See *lead swinger*.

swipe
To steal. Originally an Americanism, it became popular at the turn of the century when used by Rudyard Kipling.

synchronization of watches

Prior to any attack or raid, officers would match the time on their watches to that carried by a runner, previously set at HQ.

tab

A staff officer, from his red tabs. Also a cigarette, usually tucked behind the ear and partially smoked, from the mid-19th-century slang 'tab' for an ear.

tack wallah

A man who was teetotal. Origin obscure.

tail up

Happy, cheerful, probably derived from the cat's or dog's habit of raising its tail when pleased.

take his name

The command given to an NCO by an officer when a man has committed a military offence.

talk wet, to

To speak nonsense.

tampered bullet

A service bullet which has had the tip cut off or blunted. Not uncommon during the early part of the war, but being found in possession of any by the enemy was a death sentence.

tank

A canteen selling alcohol.

tank

Armoured fighting vehicles introduced on the Somme in September 1916. Females were armed with four machine guns, males had two 6-pdr guns and two machine guns. In their early form they were slow, unreliable and

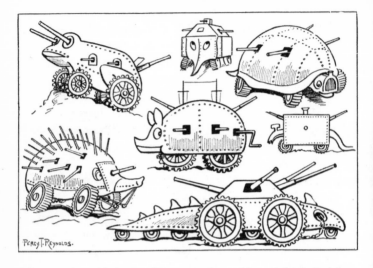

A few conceptions, picked up from Press accounts here and there, of what the "tanks" are really like. (Punch)

always vulnerable to artillery although later models were much improved. They proved to be the only means of destroying the vast belts of German barbed wire and became a vital part of the allied war effort.

tap
A wound, usually a light one. See also *Blighty one*.

taped
White tapes laid in No-Man's Land for infantry to follow during an attack. As they clearly showed the way, the word became used to also describe very accurate machine-gun or shellfire. 'Fritz has got this trench taped.'

tapped   Mad. An abbreviated form of *doolaley tap*.

tart   A prostitute. In its original form in the 1860s, it could be used as a form of endearment, but by the turn of the century it had harder connotations.

Tassie, a   A soldier from Tasmania.

taube   A pigeon or dove. The first mass-produced German two-seater monoplane, the 1910 Model Rumpler Taube, took its name from the resemblance of its wing shape to that of the bird. By 1914 they were already obsolete.

taxi-driver   A self-deprecating Royal Flying Corps term for a pilot.

tea-leaf   Thief.

tear gas   The soldiers name for *lachrymatory gas*.

tear up for arse paper   To be disciplined verbally and severely. Mainly a New Zealand expression.

teddy bears   The issue goatskin jackets.

telling a tale   Trying to explain away a mistake, or telling a woeful story.

temporary gentleman   A wry newspaper term for any civilian who became an officer. Gentleman was a word dating back at least to the early 17th century, meaning a man of good family, impeccable personal conduct and courteous manners. To be considered one was deemed of great importance. Even today it retains connotations of class superiority.

terps
An interpreter. Most regiments had an interpreter attached to them.

terrier crop
An army haircut, not from the nickname for the Territorials but from the short hair on the dog of the same name.

Terriers, the
Any Territorial Army regiment, generally a pre-1914 word.

thick
In close association or familiar. Certainly used by the mid-18th century, 'thick as thieves' being an example. Its later use, mostly by officers, dates from a century later, when 'thick' was used to denote something that was intolerable or unpleasant. 'Two patrols in a day is a bit thick.'

thigh boots
See *trench waders*.

thingummyjig
An indeterminate object. See also *ooja or oojah*, *wotsit*.

third man
A superstition that it was unlucky or fatal to light a third cigarette from the same match. In fact, there was an element of truth in this, for the average sniper required about three seconds to locate a target, aim and fire, and that was about the time it took to light three cigarettes. If this seems far fetched, it must be

remembered that a flaring match was clearly visible in the dark from a mile away – and most trenches were on average only 200 yards apart.

three blue lights
A running joke with soldiers was that the end of the war would be signalled at night with three blue flares, which would be quite invisible.

Three-Oh-Three
The standard .303in British service rifle cartridge.

throw one's weight about
To try to assert authority or intimidate others. Probably from circus language, early 1900s.

thumbs up
One of the most iconic gestures of the British soldier, it denoted a wide range of emotions, all based on pleasure, happiness or satisfaction. Although it supposedly dates back to the 'pollice verso' gesture to determine the fate of Roman gladiators, there is actually little evidence to prove this either way. It has since become a visual metaphor in English.

ticket
An official discharge from the army, normally on medical grounds. To *work one's ticket* was to maintain a façade of fake symptoms to effect a discharge, very difficult to achieve.

Tickler's
A brand of jam, almost always plum and apple, issued in tins. Soldiers grew very weary of it and longed for any other type of fruit.

	Unsurprisingly after the war Tickler's went out of business. See also *plum and apple*.
Tickler's artillery	Home-made grenades manufactured from jam tins, packed with guncotton, pieces of shell splinter or metal scrap and ignited by a simple burning fuse. More sophisticated examples had dry-cotton primer as an explosive, several rounds of .303in ammunition and a clay packing. They became obsolete with the introduction of the *Mills grenade*.
Ticky	Lousy.
tic-tacs	Army signallers. From the arm movements of the tick-tack bookmakers at horse races.
tiddlewinks	An officer's expression, with a wide range of meanings: something that was of no importance, or little consequence or eliciting sympathy. 'I'm at the OP all day tomorrow.' 'Oh, tiddlewinks old man.' Probably taken from the children's game.
tight	Drunk. Although originally meaning hard or difficult to come by, as in 'money is tight' it had by the mid-1840s also become a synonym for drunk. See also *binge, blanked, blind, blotto, pissed, squiffy, zig-zag*.
tile	A hat, from civilian slang *c.* 1820.

	Possibly analogous of a roof tile. See also *tit-for-tat*.
time serving man	A man who had voluntarily enlisted for a specific period. See also *seven*.
tin hat	The most common expression for the Brody shrapnel helmet, first issued in mid-1915. It closely resembled the medieval kettle hat. Various improvements were made to the original design and it remained in service until the end of 1945. Also known as *battle bowler*, *lid*, *pot*, *pudding basin*, *steel jug*.
tin opener	The bayonet. Seldom used for fighting, it was more often employed as a skewer for cooking, or hook to hang equipment on. Also *toasting fork*, *tooth pick*, *winkle pin*.
tin town	A camp of *corrugated iron* huts.
tit-for-tat	A hat. Usually abbreviated to 'titfer'.
TMB	trench mortar battery.
toad	The German M.1915 Discushandgranate. Its odd discus-like shape lent itself to the nickname 'toad' or 'turtle' grenade.
toasting fork	The bayonet. See also *tin opener*, *tooth pick*, *winkle pin*.
Toc H	Talbot House, from the signals alphabet. It was a rest and recreation house founded in December 1915 at Poperinghe in Belgium and named in

memory of Gilbert Talbot, killed in Ypres in July of that year, and the son of the Bishop of Winchester. The founders were Gilbert's brother Neville and the Reverend P.T.B. 'Tubby' Clayton. It was an 'Every Man's Club', where all soldiers were welcome, regardless of rank or religion. It is still in existence today.

toffee apple   See *plum pudding*.

tom tit   Shit.

Tommy   The universal term for the British soldier. Its exact origin is unclear; it was used as early as 1743 in a letter sent to England from the British forces in Jamaica. It became much popularized in 1899 when a poem written by a Private Smith of the Black Watch was published (see Appendix 4). Newspapers of the Great War began to use it as a generic term as did French and German soldiers but the British soldier seldom used it. Today many serving soldiers refer to themselves at 'Toms'.

tommy bar   A short hooked bar used to remove the ring and split pin from *Mills grenades*. Now it is a universal term for any extension bar to provide additional leverage.

tommy bread   Used by the regular army it was a civilian term for food, bread in particular, often supplied to workmen in lieu of wages.

tommy cooker   A small folding stove that used a solid alcohol cube much like a firelighter. Mostly useless unless additional combustible material was added.

toodle-pip   A farewell, mostly officers' slang. See also *be good*, *cheer-o*, *chin-chin*.

toot sweet   Quickly, from the French 'tout de suite'.

tooth pick   The bayonet. Sometimes simply 'pick'. See also *tin opener*, *toasting fork*, *winkle pin*.

Top of the Shop   99 in the game of *House*.

tot   A measure of 1/64th of a gallon, or ½ gill.

touch   To try to obtain a favour. 'I'll touch the new corporal for a fag later.'

touched   Mad or eccentric. Possibly from a 19th-century southern costermongers' expression for vegetables that were going bad. See also *dippy*, *doolally*, *tapped*.

toughs, the   A group of men who regarded themselves as superior, and able to bear hardships, used a little like *the heads*. Its origin is probably Canadian, where it was a term for endurance or ability to face hardships, i.e. 'Tough things out'. Post-war it was used to refer to a man of a criminal disposition. Also the nickname of the Royal Dublin Fusiliers.

tour
The time spent in the line, either at the front or in reserve. Usually this was between four and six days, depending on the sector. Sometimes also called 'trench duty'.

town major
An officer who was seldom more senior than a captain stationed in a town or large village, whose responsibility it was to find accommodation for troops in transit. A demanding and thankless job.

tracers
Bullets that contained an illuminating compound that enabled their trajectory to be followed. Mostly used in aircraft, but later in the war they were sometimes used by ground machine guns to judge range.

tractor
An aeroplane with the propeller at the front. See also *pusher*.

transport lines
The area behind the line from where wagon transport went forward to deliver stores to the front lines.

traverse
The partition separating the *fire bays*, giving protection from shell blast and preventing the enemy from enfilading the trench with small arms fire. See also *fire bay*, *trench*.

traversing
Moving a muzzle of a machine gun slowly from side to side to sweep the ground in front with fire.

trek

A forced march, from the Afrikaans/ Dutch 'voortrekkers', emigrants who walked into the interior of Southern Africa to colonize it in the 1830s.

trench

A deep ditch, acting as a line of defence and shelter. They consisted of *fire bays* and *traverses* and were typically over 6ft deep, where ground conditions permitted them to be dug. By 1915 the trench lines on the Western Front stretched unbroken from the Channel to the Swiss border, some 450 miles. See also *reserve trench*, *support trench*.

trench club

Of many and varied designs, it was a heavy, short wooden shaft with an iron weight or lead infill at one end. Simpler ones were merely studded with hobnails. Crude, but very effective for *trench raids*. See also *knobkerrie*.

trench fever

Also known as the 'five day fever', it remained a mystery until it was realized it was transmitted by body lice. It affected about a quarter of the armies on the Western Front. Recovery took a month or more. See *PUO*.

trench foot

Constant immersion in wet, cold water caused the flesh to rot, leading in untreated cases to gangrene. Contracting it was made a military crime which did little to remedy the problem. In an attempt to prevent it, *whale oil* was issued. During the Falklands War of 1982 soldiers still suffered from it.

trench mortar A short-barrelled artillery piece of small to moderate calibre, that fired a shell almost vertically. This made them particularly lethal as they dropped straight into trenches. Some of the larger ones could cause considerable damage. See *flying pig*, *Minnie*, *plum pudding*, *Stokes mortar*.

trench mouth A painful swelling of the gums, due to eating food contaminated with bacteria, and an inability to wash one's hands before handling it.

trench raid These were organized raids on a small section of enemy front, usually in order to capture prisoners and information. Often very risky undertakings, they were taken seriously by the staff, and disliked intensely by the soldiers.

trench ring A finger ring made from any suitable piece of war scrap.

trench stores The items that remained in a trench when one battalion took over from another. They included *trench waders*, *Very lights*, grenade dumps, etc.

trench waders	Also *thigh boots*. Long, thigh-length rubber boots that were issued to help keep feet dry, and were worn over the issue boot.
trey bon	Very good, from the French 'tres bon'. Also used as 'trey bon for the troops' for anything that was regarded as generally acceptable. See also *bon*.
trip wire	Either a wire laid close to the ground in No-Man's Land to ensnare patrols, or a wire linked to a booby-trap, often a grenade.
trooper	A cavalry soldier.
troops, the	A soldier's light-hearted form of self-address. 'Cor, the troops could do with a rum ration.'
trouble and strife	Wife.
truce	A temporary cessation of hostilities on a local level, usually to bury the dead or collect the wounded.
trumpet cleaning, gone	Dead.
tube or tube train	A very heavy shell passing overhead, from the sound.
Tug	Any man called Wilson, possibly (though not conclusively) after Admiral of the Fleet Sir Arthur Knyvet Wilson VC (4 March 1842–25 May 1921) who once ignored naval etiquette and offered the captain of a battleship a 'tug'.
tumble down the sink	To drink, often shortened to 'tumble'.

turd walloper	Sanitary man.
tutoring	Time spent showing new soldiers the routines of trench life.
Two Five Two	Army form 252, on which men's crimes were recorded.
'U' frame	A wooden framework used to reinforce trench walls. Also a variant as 'A' frame.
uckeye	From the Hindi for all right, or acceptable. This is an interesting word, for the etymology of the term 'OK' has long been ascribed to its introduction in the United States in the early 19th century. However, it was used in the British Army from its earliest days policing the Indian Empire in the 18th century and 'uckeye' may well be the origin of the now universally known term.
umpteen	Many, a lot. Introduced during the war it does not define any specific number.
umpty iddy	To feel. To be unwell, although the original term meant to be drunk.
umpty poo	To ask for more, from the French 'un petit peu'.
Uncle Ned	Bed.
undertakers or undertaker's squad	See *stretcher bearers*.
Unhealthy	Dangerous, usually of a place under shell or sniper fire. Another typical British understatement.

Unknown Warrior

Immediately after the war, it was decided that one anonymous soldier should represent the tens of thousands who had no known grave. Six unidentified corpses from the RFC, Royal Naval Division (RND) and army were selected from Western Front battlefields, placed in identical coffins and a blindfolded senior officer selected one at random. The Unknown Warrior was buried in Westminster Abbey on 11 November 1920. The full inscription on the headstone can be found in Appendix 5.

up for the office

Called to the orderly room.

up the line

To head to the front lines, whether it be from a base camp or rest billet.

up there, it's

Showing, usually with a finger tapping the side of the head, that the man in question is a successful *scrounger*, can *swing the lead* or has simply scored a small victory against army bureaucracy.

VAD

Voluntary Aid Detachment. Volunteer nurses who were prepared to serve overseas. 74,000 volunteered in 1914, and two-thirds were female.

valise

The officer's equivalent of a *knapsack* for infantrymen. It was a large canvas kitbag containing all his personal effects, normally carried on a *messcart*.

vamoose
To leave quickly. From the Spanish 'vamos', let's go. Adopted by British troops garrisoning Gibraltar, probably as early as the 18th century and in use in London by the mid-1800s.

van blank
White wine, 'vin blanc'.

VC mixture
The rum issue. See also *SRD*.

velvet, to be on
In an easy or advantageous position. In civilian use in the south of England by late 18th century.

Vermorel sprayer
A commercial rose-sprayer, they were filled with Hypo Soda to aid dispersal of low-lying gas in trenches. Sometimes also filled with a solution to kill insects.

Very light or Very flare
A pyrotechnic cartridge, about the size of a 12-bore shotgun, that was fired from a smooth-bored pistol. It launched a bright flare that could be used for signalling, or a small *parachute flare* that descended slowly and illuminated the surrounding vicinity.

Very pistol
A large barrelled single shot pistol for firing flares. Named after its inventor, Edward W. Very, an American naval officer.

vet, the
The medical officer.

vetted
Medically examined. By the end of

	the war also to have been examined or questioned verbally.
Vickers	The Vickers Machine Gun, manufactured by the Vickers Company of Erith, Kent, was the standard .303-cal. medium machine gun of the Great War. It was almost identical in function to the German Maxim gun.
VC	Victoria Cross. See Appendix 6.
Vlam	Vlamertinghe in Flanders.
WAAC	Women's Army Auxiliary Corps, pronounced 'Wacks'. Roughly corresponding to *VADs* except that they wore *khaki* uniforms. They performed clerical work in base camps and were always the butt of ribald humour.
wad	A canteen sandwich or bun.
wag	A humorist or joker. Every battalion had their share.
walking wounded	Men who were wounded but still mobile enough to walk.
wallah	A man, or fellow. From the Hindi word 'wala' meaning connected to. Hence *base wallah*, char wallah etc.
wangle	Much the same as *scrounge* but perhaps a little more official. 'I showed the QM my torn shirt and managed to wangle a new one out of him.'

First Officer (in spasm of jealousy). "Who's the knock-knee chap with your sister, old man?"
Second Officer. "My other sister." (Punch)

war babies Children born out of liaisons between French or Belgian women and allied soldiers. Also a 'war baby', which was a youthful junior officer.

war on, there's a A phrase used by both soldiers and civilians alluding to the fact that the demands of war required certain sacrifices, or priorities. Also much used in the Second World War.

wash-out The failure of either a person or thing, often applied to military operations. From the mid-19th-century shooting term, where a wash-out meant to completely miss the target.

wastage	A military term for men killed or wounded during ordinary trench duty. On average this was 15 men per battalion, per day.
Waterloo Day	Pay day.
waterproof sheet	A rubberized green ground sheet that could be worn as a poncho, attached to others to form a make-shift tent or placed on the ground to sit on. They also doubled up as *gas sheets*. Considered a vital part of a soldier's kit.
wear	To put up with, a regular army expression.
Weary Willie	A high, slow-moving shell that moaned as it passed overhead.
webbing	A close-woven cotton that produced a very strong dense material used for belts, ammunition pouches, *knapsacks* etc. The British Army adopted webbing equipment in 1908.
weigh up	To appraise a situation or person. From the boxing term, where a man would be weighed up prior to a bout.
well oiled	Very drunk.
West spring gun	A piece of mechanical absurdity invented by Captain Allen West in 1915 that resembled the medieval trebuchet. It weighed 300lb and was designed to hurl *Mills grenades* 80 yards.

west, to go

To be killed, but also of a thing that was lost or failed to work. 'The engine's gone west.' Its origin is obscure, but it was first recorded in the 16th century when referring to prisoners who had been hanged and it possibly refers to the finality of the sun setting in the west.

wet behind the ears

Ignorant, untrained or inexperienced.

whack

An equal share, dating back to the Napoleonic wars.

whacked or whacked out

Exhausted, the same as *beat*.

whale oil

Issued as an evil-smelling grease it was supposed to help prevent *trench foot*. As soldiers invariably had to put wet socks and boots back on, it was of little help.

what hopes

An expression of disbelief. 'The war will end this month. What hopes!'

Whippet

A much lighter, faster tank than the Mk IV, introduced in December 1917. It had a three-man crew.

whistle and flute

A suit.

Whistling Percy

Specifically, a German 9in high-velocity naval gun captured at Cambrai in 1917.

white feather

As a sign of cowardice, some women handed these to men who were not in uniform, occasionally risking the wrath of wounded

	soldiers or reserved occupation men who were in 'civvies'. See also *conscientious objector, conshie*.
White-sheets	Wytschaete in Flanders.
whizz-bang	A fast, light artillery shell (18-pdr, 75mm or 77mm) that gave virtually no warning of its approach.
widow's mite	A light.
wilkie, a	A playing card, from the name of a popular musical hall comedian, Wilkie Bard.
win	Much the same a *scrounge*, it usually meant that the current owner hadn't actually asked the previous one if he could have the item.
wind-up, to have the	Fear. All soldiers had it, but managed to conquer it most of the time. There is no consensus as to its origin.
windy	Similar to the above, but also used as a comment about another man. 'He's too windy to go on that raid tonight.'
Windy Corner	There were several places on the Western Front with this name, usually due to the heavy shellfire they attracted.
winkle out	To persuade a defender to leave his *dug-out* and surrender. From the act of using a pin to extract winkles from their shells.

winkle pin
Bayonet. Sometimes simply 'pin'. See also *tin opener*, *toasting fork*, *tooth pick*.

Wipers
The most popular pronunciation of *Ypres*.

Wipers Express
A huge 42cm shell that the Germans used during the second battle of Ypres (21 April–25 May 1915) from the sound it made as it passed overhead.

Wipers Times
A satirical trench magazine first produced in Ypres in February 1916 by Captain F. Roberts and Lieutenant J. Pearson of the Notts and Derby Regiment. The final issue was printed in December 1918.

wire cutters
Used to snip the German barbed wire prior to an attack. Of many different types, they had to have wide jaws, as German wire was much thicker than British.

wiring party
The men responsible for laying barbed wire in No-Man's Land. An unpopular but necessary fatigue, done under cover of darkness.

WO
Either the War Office or, more frequently, the regimental sergeant major who was a warrant officer.

Women's Legion
Civilian volunteers who mostly drove cars and lorries.

wonky
Spurious, inferior or damaged. A printer's term from *c*. 1900.

Woodbine
A cheap and popular brand of cigarette. Newspaper reports had the public believing that it was the only cigarette ever smoked by the troops.

Woodbine Willy
Geoffrey Studdert Kennedy, (1883–1929) was a chaplain on the Western Front. His preference for sharing front-line life and inexhaustible supply of cigarettes earned him the admiration of the soldiers. He won the MC for rescuing a wounded man under fire.

wooden overcoat
A coffin. Dating back at least to the 18th century.

woolly bear
An German airburst shrapnel shell, usually of 15cm, that exploded in a large cloud of fluffy brown smoke.

work one's ticket
See *ticket*.

working party
Any group of soldiers detailed for fatigues such as filling in shell holes, repairing trenches etc. Slightly different to the job of a *ration party*.

wotsit
An indeterminate object. See also *ooja or oojah*, *thingummyjig*.

wound stripe
The gold bar(s) worn on the left sleeve. See also *gold stripes*.

WRAF
Women's Royal Air Force. Generally known as 'Wraffs' they wore blue uniforms and served as chauffeurs and clerical staff.

wristwatch

Quite a novelty in the early years of the war when most watches were of the fob type. A wristwatch was a greatly prized *souvenir*.

write off

To be completely destroyed. Initially an airforce expression relating to a crashed aircraft, it was soon adopted by all services. From the physical act of crossing a destroyed item off a list of serviceable aeroplanes.

WRNS

Women's Royal Naval Service. Known as 'Wrens' they acted as drivers and clerks.

yellow cross shell

A sulphur-mustard gas shell used by the Germans. See also *blue cross shell, gas, green cross shell*.

Ypres

The town in Flanders surrounded by the infamous Salient. It was the epicentre of four years of fighting and became a byword for the most awful conditions to be found anywhere on the Western Front. It was totally destroyed during the fighting, but reconstructed post-war. See also *Eeepray or Eeeps, Wipers*.

Z

Short for Zero Hour, the time normally designated for the start of an attack. Sometimes also 'Zero Day'.

Zeppelin in the clouds

Sausage and mash.

zero

To match, or collimate, the point of impact of a bullet with the point of aim of the rifles' sights, and adjust the sights accordingly. Usually a sniper's term.

zig-zag, a   A drunk. From the wobbly walk of a man full of alcohol. See also *binge*, *blanked*, *blind*, *blotto*, *pissed*, *squiffy*, *tight*.

PART 2
SOLDIERS' SONGS

POPULAR SONGS

I t is almost impossible to exaggerate the importance of song in the armies of 1914–18. Few things could raise the morale of soldiers like singing, and the army actively encouraged it, with the use of traditional marching tunes. In fact, the songs of the early 20th century played a far greater part in British culture than today, for pre-war, almost all music was heard live, in music or concert halls and vaudeville theatres. Only the wealthier elements of society owned record players so most ordinary people learned songs at first hand. A great deal of this music was sung and played by amateurs at private gatherings, where accompaniment by piano was the only additional music. The medium by which this happened was sheet music, now virtually relegated to the dustbin of history by modern recording methods. To provide some idea of the size of the commercial market for printed music, 'It's A Long Way To Tipperary', when released in 1914, was selling at the rate of 10,000 musical scores *per day*.

During the rare times when people were not working, the most popular venues were the music halls and variety theatres. They were cheap, easy for working people to reach and had acts that encompassed everything; from poetic recitals to scantily clad dancing girls, and they provided the primary form of enjoyment for the working classes. Artists such as George Robey, Oscar Asche, Marie Lloyd and Vesta Tilley were household names and became rich and famous as a result. There was another side to the music halls though, for the government quickly realized that they provided a vital and powerful platform for recruitment and as a means of disseminating propaganda. Some performers, most notably Vesta Tilley and her impresario husband, actually pioneered much of this stage-based recruiting. 'Vesta Tilley was on stage. She was beautifully dressed in a lovely gown of gold or silver. But what we didn't know until we got there was that also on stage were army officers with tables all set up for recruiting. She introduced those songs: "We Don't Want To Lose You" and "Rule Britannia" ... then she came off the stage and walked all around the audience ... and the young men were getting up and following her. She put her hands on my husband's shoulder – and as the men were all following her, he got up and followed her too.'[*]

Songs were a traditional means of entertainment in every walk of life and naturally the soldiers were no exception. But the war brought with it a schism in the social fabric of the country and a gradual but forceful

---

[*] Kitty Eckersley, quoted in *Forgotten Voices Of The Great War*, Max Arthur, Ebury Press, London, 2002.

shift in public attitude towards the fighting and how it was represented in popular culture. Uniquely, civilians who were not in the combat areas became deliberate targets when the Germans bombarded Scarborough, Hartlepool and Whitby in December 1914 and Zeppelin raids began in January 1915. The level of fear and panic this generated is hard to understand now and scared Londoners took refuge in the tube stations in huge numbers. Singing was almost the only morale defence they had. 'The men calmed the fears of the women, and after a time stolid British silence was the prevailing note among the people. Popular songs were started, and soon the stations were echoing to the rollicking choruses.'*

The music halls and theatres were as much a reflection of contemporary attitudes as they were places of entertainment and as the war progressed the public, and soldiers on leave, began to feel uncomfortable about what was increasingly being seen as no more than thinly disguised propaganda. Many of the songs that had been popular in 1914 were no longer acceptable a year later. In the list of the best-selling songs of 1915, published annually by Francis and Day, there was not one recruiting song. As the war progressed, this growing cynicism forced a change in musical tastes. Many of the better composers recognized this, Bennett Scott writing that 'I have to explain [to my publisher] that what went in 1910 won't go in 1916.'** Initially these songs had been jingoistic and rousing, 'Pack Up Your Troubles' being a

---

* *Daily Mail*, Tuesday 25 September 1917.

** R.A. Baker, *British Music Hall, An Illustrated History*, Sutton, Stroud, 2005, p.169.

fine example, but after the carnage of 1916, war-weariness altered the mood of the songs. It was no coincidence that this happened almost in parallel to the work of the war poets, whose early war jingoism had also changed to a darker, more critical tone.

New satirical tunes like 'They Were Only Playing Leapfrog' underlined the disparity between the life of the senior officers and that of the rank and file and were becoming increasingly numerous. Particularly popular were parodies of existing songs; 'When This Bloody War Is Over', was sung to the tune of a popular hymn, 'What A Friend We Have In Jesus'. 'Never Mind' was a cynical version of a pre-war song called 'Though Your Heart May Ache Awhile' and 'I Wore A Tunic' was aimed directly at men avoiding service at home, whilst 'Hanging On The Old Barbed Wire' was a truly barbed criticism of the callousness of war.

Many current songs were sung in the front lines by amateur theatrical groups who performed at the popular divisional concerts. Familiar pre-war songs like 'Let's All Go Down The Strand' or 'Daisy Bell' evoked a sense of home and familiarity, and war-related songs, such as 'Roses Of Picardy' became national favourites but it was stage revues that became the most influential in terms of providing popular melodies. There were musicals of many differing types: *The Bing Boys Are Here* (April 1916) was a revue, and *Chu-Chin-Chow* (August 1916) was described as 'an adult pantomime', whilst *The Maid of the Mountains* (January 1917) was a light operetta. They gave the world songs such as 'If You Were The Only Girl In the World' and 'A Paradise For Two' and propelled their performers to stardom. Officers and soldiers on leave regarded seeing the latest productions as obligatory, and tens of thousands went to see them. 'One of my earliest theatrical memories is seeing Oscar Asche in *Chu-Chin-Chow*... I was overwhelmed by the production ... the troops who were home on leave from the trenches, adored *Chu-Chin-Chow*. The theatre was full of khaki and blue.'* Post-1917, more American show and commercially written songs began to appear, notably the rousing and optimistic 'Over There' and these added a new, and more upbeat element to the soldier's repertoire.

---

* John Gielgud, *An Actor and His Time*, Sidgwick and Jackson, London, 1979, p.23. The reference to blue was the wounded men in their hospital blue uniforms.

'Love's Old Sweet Song', 1884

Music: J.L. Molloy. Lyrics: G. Clifton Bingham

Sometimes better known as 'Just A Song At Twilight', it was an extremely popular Victorian parlour-song and during the war spawned many parodies.

Once in the dear dead days beyond recall,
When on the world the mists began to fall,
Out of the dreams that rose in happy throng,
Low to our hearts Love sang an old sweet song;
And in the dusk where fell the firelight gleam,
Softly it wove itself into our dream.

CHORUS:
Just a song at twilight, when the lights are low,
And the flick'ring shadows softly come and go,
Tho' the heart be weary, sad the day and long,
Still to us at twilight comes Love's old song,
Comes Love's old sweet song.

Even today we hear Love's song of yore,
Deep in our hearts it dwells forevermore.
Footsteps may falter, weary grow the way,
Still we can hear it at the close of day.
So till the end, when life's dim shadows fall,
Love will be found the sweetest song of all.

REPEAT CHORUS.

'Where Did You Get That Hat?' 1888

Music and lyrics: J.J. Sullivan

A light-hearted ditty using popular slang that was meaningful in an era when every man wore a hat of some sort. At least one infantry battalion in France, having marched past a general with his resplendent gold-braided cap, burst forth with this song.

Where did you get that hat,
Where did you get that tile?
Isn't it a knobby one
In just the proper style?
I should like to have one
Just the same as that.
Where e'er I go they shout
'Hello, where did you get that hat?'

Now how I came to get this hat
Is very strange and funny.
My uncle died and left to me
His property and money.
And when the will it was read out,
They told me straight and flat,
If I'm to have his money I must also wear his hat.

When I go to the concert hall,
In the concert season
Someone's sure to shout at me,
Without the slightest reason.
When I go to the opera hall,

To have a jolly spree,
There's one or two sopranos,
Who are sure to shout at me,
'Hello, where did you get that hat?'

When Mr And Mrs Ramsbottom
Had their last garden party,
I was amongst the guests,
Who had a welcome true and hearty.
The Prince of Wales was also there,
And my heart jumped with glee,
When someone said the prince
Would like to have a word with me,
'Hello, where did you get that hat?'

'Ta-Ra-Ra Boom-De-Ay', 1891

Music and lyrics attributed to Henry Sayers. New lyrics:
Richard Morton

Although an American tune, its actual history is shrouded in confusion. Originally attributed to an American stage show called *Tuxedo*, it was allegedly re-written by Morton and performed in London in 1892 in a music hall at the Tivoli, in the form below.

A smart and stylish girl you see,
Belle of good society,
Not too strict but rather free,
Yet as right as right can be!
Never forward, never bold,

Not too hot, and not too cold,
But the very thing, I'm told,
That in your arms you'd like to hold.

CHORUS:
Ta-ra-ra boom-de-ay! *(sung eight times)*

I'm not extravagantly shy,
And when a nice young man is nigh,
For his heart I have a try,
And faint away with tearful cry!
When the good young man in haste,
Will support me round the waist,
I don't come to while thus embraced,
Till of my lips he steals a taste!

REPEAT CHORUS.

I'm a timid flow'r of innocence,
Pa says that that I have no sense,
I'm one eternal big expense,
But men say that I'm just 'immense'!
Ere my verses I conclude,
I'd like it known and understood,
Though free as air, I'm never rude,
I'm not too bad and not too good!

REPEAT CHORUS.

You should see me out with Pa,
Prim, and most particular;
The young men say, 'Ah, there you are!'

And Pa says, 'That's peculiar!'
'It's like their cheek!' I say, and so
Off again with Pa I go –
He's quite satisfied – although,
When his back's turned – well, you know –

REPEAT CHORUS.

'Daisy Bell (A Bicycle Built For Two)', 1892

Music and lyrics: Harry Dacre

When Dacre emigrated from Britain to the United States he took his bicycle with him, and was charged import duty. A friend remarked that it was a good job it wasn't a bicycle built for two, otherwise he'd have to pay double. Dacre thought this such a charming phrase, he wrote this song about it. It was hugely popular with troops throughout the war.

There is a flower within my heart,
Daisy, Daisy!
Planted one day by a glancing dart,
Planted by Daisy Bell!
Whether she loves me or loves me not,
Sometimes it's hard to tell;
Yet I am longing to share the lot
Of beautiful Daisy Bell!

CHORUS:
Daisy Daisy,

Give me your answer do!
I'm half crazy,
All for the love of you!
It won't be a stylish marriage,
I can't afford a carriage,
But you'll look sweet upon the seat
Of a bicycle built for two!

We will go tandem as man and wife,
Daisy, Daisy!
Ped'ling away down the road of life,
I and my Daisy Bell!
When the road's dark we can despise
P'liceman and lamps as well;
There are bright lights in the dazzling eyes
Of beautiful Daisy Bell!

REPEAT CHORUS.

I will stand by you in 'wheel' or woe,
Daisy, Daisy!
You'll be the belle which I ring, you know!
Sweet little Daisy Bell!
You'll take the lead in each trip we take,
Then if I don't do well;
I will permit you to use the brake,
My beautiful Daisy Bell!

REPEAT CHORUS.

'Oh, Mr Porter', 1893

Music and lyrics: George Le Brun

One of Marie Lloyd's showstoppers, it was performed throughout her stage career and became one of the most popular stage songs of the period.

Lately I just spent a week with my old Aunt Brown,

Came up to see wond'rous sights of famous London Town.

Just a week I had of it, all round the place we'd roam,

Wasn't I sorry on the day I had to go back home?

Worried about with packing, I arrived late at the station,

Dropped my hatbox in the mud, the things all fell about,

Got my ticket, said, 'good-bye'. 'Right away,' the guard did cry.

But I found the train was wrong and shouted out:

CHORUS:

Oh! Mister Porter, what shall I do?

I want to go to Birmingham,

And they're taking me on to Crewe,

Send me back to London as quickly as you can,

Oh! Mister Porter, what a silly girl I am!

The porter would not stop the train, but I laughed and said, 'You must

Keep your hair on, Mary Ann, and mind that you don't bust.'

Some old gentleman inside declared that it was hard,

Said, 'Look out of the window, Miss, and try and call the guard.'

Didn't I, too, with all my might I nearly balanced over,

But my old friend grasp'd my leg, and pulled me back again,

Nearly fainting with the fright, I sank into his arms a sight,

Went into hysterics but I cried in vain:

REPEAT CHORUS.

On his clean old shirt-front then I laid my trembling head,
'Do take it easy, rest awhile,' the dear old chappie said.
If you make a fuss of me and on me do not frown,
You shall have my mansion, dear, away in London Town.
Wouldn't you think me silly if I said I could not like him?
Really he seemed a nice old boy, so I replied this way;
'I will be your own for life, Your imay doodle um little wife,
If you'll never tease me any more I say.'

REPEAT CHORUS.

'Goodbye Dolly Grey', 1898

Music: Paul Barnes. Lyrics: Will Cobb

Hugely sentimental, it was written by Americans Barnes and Cobb during the Spanish–American War of 1898. However, it achieved national popularity in England during the later Boer War (1899–1902) where it virtually became an anthem, and was revived in 1914.

I have come to say goodbye, Dolly Gray,
It's no use to ask me why, Dolly Gray,
There's a murmur in the air, you can hear it everywhere,
It's the time to do and dare, Dolly Gray – so
Goodbye Dolly I must leave you, though it breaks my heart to go,
Something tells me I am needed at the front to fight the foe,
See – the soldier boys are marching and I can no longer stay,
Hark – I hear the bugle calling, goodbye Dolly Gray.

Can't you hear the sound of feet, Dolly Gray,

Marching through the village street, Dolly Gray,

That's the tramp of soldiers' feet in their uniforms so neat,

So – goodbye until we meet, Dolly Gray. Goodbye Dolly Gray.

'Nellie Dean', 1905

Music and lyrics: Henry W. Armstrong

Although a song with a chorus beloved by amiable drunks, the character Nellie Dean was actually the primary narrator in Emily Brontë's *Wuthering Heights* but the lyrics bear no relationship to the story. Often sung lustily by soldiers in estaminets and canteens.

By the old mill stream I'm dreaming, Nellie Dean;

Dreaming of your bright eyes gleaming, Nellie Dean.

As they used to fondly glow,

When we sat there long ago,

List'ning to the waters flow, Nellie Dean.

I can hear the robins singing, Nellie Dean;

Sweetest recollections bringing, Nellie Dean.

And they seem to sing of you,

With your tender eyes of blue,

For I know they miss you too, Nellie Dean.

CHORUS:

There's an old mill by the stream, Nellie Dean,

Where we used to sit and dream, Nellie Dean.

And the waters as they flow,

Seem to murmur sweet and low,
You're my heart's desire; I love you, Nellie Dean.

I recall the day we parted, Nellie Dean;
How you trembled broken hearted, Nellie Dean.
And you pinned a rose of red
On my coat of blue and said,
That a soldier boy you'd wed, Nellie Dean.
All the world seems sad and lonely, Nellie Dean;
For I love you and you only, Nellie Dean.
And I wonder if on high,
You still love me, if you sigh
For the happy days gone by, Nellie Dean

REPEAT CHORUS.

'I Do Like To Be Beside The Seaside', 1907

Music and lyrics: John A. Glover-Kind

Written at a time when many working class families were able to visit the coast for the first time, it was a great favourite in music halls. Mark Sheridan (composer of 'Belgium Put The Kibosh On The Kaiser') made this his signature song, and was primarily responsible for it becoming a national hit. It was frequently sung with some humour by the soldiers when on the march.

Oh! I do like to be beside the seaside,
I do like to be beside the sea!
I do like to stroll along the Prom, Prom, Prom!

Where the brass bands play:
'Tiddely-om-pom-pom!'

So just let me be beside the seaside,
I'll be beside myself with glee.
And there's lots of girls beside,
I should like to be beside,
Beside the seaside!
Beside the sea!

'Has Anybody Here Seen Kelly?' 1908

Music: C.W. Murphy. Lyrics: Will Letters

A song by Florrie Ford, very popular at the front where it was often sung by two sections of men, one the refrain, the other the chorus.

Kelly and his sweetheart wore a very pleasant smile,
And sent upon a holiday they went from Mona's Isle,
They landed safe in London but alas it's sad to say,
For Kelly lost his little girl up Piccadilly way.
She searched for him in vain and then of course began to fret,
And this is the appeal she made to everyone she met:

CHORUS:
Has anybody here seen Kelly?
K-E-double-L-Y.
Has anybody here seen Kelly?
Find him if you can!
He's as bad as old Antonio,

Left me on my own-ee-o,

Has anybody here seen Kelly?

Kelly from the Isle of Man!

When it started raining she exclaimed, 'What shall I do?'

For Kelly had her ticket and her spending money too,

She wandered over London like a hound upon the scent,

At last she found herself outside the Houses of Parliament.

She got among the suffragettes who chained her to the grille,

And soon they heard her shouting in a voice both loud and shrill:

REPEAT CHORUS.

'I Wonder Who's Kissing Her Now', 1909

Music: Joseph Howard and Harold Orlob. Lyrics: Will M. Hough and Frank R. Adams

From the 1909 musical *Prince Of Tonight*. It was a song that reflected the age-old concerns of soldiers away from home, who had left their wives and sweethearts behind.

You have loved lots of girls in the sweet long ago,

And each one has meant Heaven to you.

You have vowed your affection to each one in turn,

And have sworn to them all you'd be true.

You have kissed 'neath the moon while the world seemed in tune,

Then you've left her to hunt a new game,

Does it ever occur to you later, my boy,

That she's probably doing the same.

CHORUS:
I wonder who's kissing her now,
Wonder who's teaching her how,
Wonder who's looking into her eyes
Breathing sighs, telling lies;

Entanglements
"COME ON, BERT, IT'S SAFER IN THE TRENCHES"
(Bruce Bairnsfather, author's collection)

I wonder who's buying the wine,
For lips that I used to call mine,
Wonder if she ever tells him of me,
I wonder who's kissing her now.

If you want to feel wretched and lonely and blue,
Just imagine the girl you love best
In the arms of some fellow who's stealing a kiss,
From the lips that you once fondly pressed.
But the world moves a pace and the loves of today,
Flit away with a smile and a tear.
So you never can tell who is kissing her now,
Or just whom you'll be kissing next year.

REPEAT CHORUS.

'Let's All Go Down The Strand', 1909

Music: Harry Casting. Lyrics: C.W. Murphy

The Strand is one of the most iconic streets in London, and this was very much a Londoner's song. The chorus was particularly popular and on one occasion was heard being sung lustily by a London battalion when up to their knees in wet mud in the line near Ypres in 1917.

One night, half a dozen tourists met together in Trafalgar Square.
A fortnight's tour on the continent was planned,
And each had his portmanteau in his hand.
Down the Rhine they meant to have a picnic,
Till Jones said, 'I must decline.

You boys have been advised by me,
Stay away from Germany,
What's the good of going down the Rhine?'

CHORUS:
Let's all go down the Strand.
Let's all go down the Strand.
I'll be leader, you can march behind,
Come with me and see what you can find.
Let's all go down the Strand.
Oh what a happy land,
That's the place for fun and noise,
All among the girls and boys.
So let's all go down the Strand.

One day five and twenty convicts
Sat in five and twenty little cells.
The bell then sounded ding-a-ding-a-dong,
To exercise the prisoners came along.
Burglar Ben exclaimed to Jaggs the Warden,
'To me sir, it's very strange.
The men are tired of going round,
Round and round the same old ground
I propose we make a little change.'

REPEAT CHORUS.

Great crowds gathered round to welcome
Shackleton returning from the Pole.
The Lord Mayor welcomed all the gallant crew,
And said, 'My lads, I've got a treat for you.
Come with me, the Mansion House awaits you.

A banquet shall be supplied.'
But a Tar in grumbling mood,
Said, 'We don't want any food.'
Then he turned to Shackleton and sighed.

REPEAT CHORUS.

These next two songs are nice examples of very specific regional songs, from East London. Both rely on Cockney rhyming slang, although the first, 'My Old Dutch', was based on an old air that was widely sung throughout the army. However, the second would have been all but incomprehensible to any but a Londoner!

'My Old Dutch', *c.* 1910

Music by: Albert Chevalier. Lyrics: A.C. Ingle

I've got a pal, a regular out an' outer.
She's a dear old gal, an' I'll tell you all about 'er;
It's forty years since fust we met,
Her hair was then as black as jet.
It's whiter now, but she don't fret,
Not my old gal.

We've been together now for forty years,
An' it don't seem a day too much.
There ain't a lady living in the land,
As I'd swap for me dear old Dutch.

No, there ain't a lady living in the land,
As I'd swap for me dear old Dutch.

'The Barrer Boy Song', c. 1910

Music: Art Noel and Frank Walsh. Lyrics: Joe Burley and Harry Bull

Up the apples and pears and across the Rory o'Moore,
Up to see me dear old trouble and strife.
On the Cain and Abel you will always see
A pair of Jack the Rippers and a cup of Rosie Lee.
What could be better than this, a bit of a cuddle and kiss
Out beneath the pale moonlight.
When little Tommy Tucker goes up to Uncle Ned
Blows out the 'Arry Randle and a jolly good night instead.

All me life I wanted to be a barrer boy,
A barrer boy I've always wanted to be.
I wheels me barrer, I pushes it with pride,
I'm a coster, a coster, from over the other side.
I turns me back on all the old society
I'm going where the ripe bananas grow.
I sells 'em a dozen a shilling, that's 'ow I makes me living,
I ought to 'ave been a barrer boy years ago.
(Get off me barrer!)
I ought to 'ave been a barrer boy years ago.

'I'm 'Enery The Eighth I Am', 1910

Music and lyrics: F. Murray and R.P. Weston

Written as a music-hall ditty and sung by Harry Champion, it was unexpectedly revived in the 1960s by Joe Brown and Herman's Hermits, and reached No. 1 in the pop charts!

I'm 'Enery the Eighth, I am,
'Enery the Eighth I am, I am!
I got married to the widow next door,
She's been married seven times before,
And every one was an 'Enery
She wouldn't have a Willie nor a Sam.
I'm her eighth old man named 'Enery
'Enery the Eighth, I am!

'Hold Your Hand Out, Naughty Boy', 1912

Music: C.W. Murphy. Lyrics: Worton David

A favourite of music hall star Florrie Ford. In France it was often sung quite suggestively by French girls on stage clad only in very basic clothing, to roars of approval from their audience.

At the club one evening Jones was telling all his pals
How much he hated girls, despised their golden curls.
'You wouldn't catch me with a girl, you bet your life,' said he.
'Girls possess no charms for me.'

Then one chap at Jones began to leer,
Picked up his cane and said, 'Come here'.

CHORUS:
Hold your hand out, naughty boy.
Hold your hand out, naughty boy.
Last night, in the pale moonlight,
I saw you, I saw you;
With a nice girl in the park,
You were strolling full of joy,
And you told here you'd never kissed a girl before:
Hold your hand out, naughty boy.

All alone to Gay Paree on business went Papa,
And when he landed back his wife said, 'Tell me Jack,
While you have been in Paris have you always thought of me?'
'Always darling,' murmured he,
'For you've been pining night and day.'
And then the gramophone began to play.

REPEAT CHORUS.

'Keep Your Head Down'

*A parody on the tune: 'Hold Your Hand Out,
Naughty Boy'.*

Keep your head down Fritzy boy,
Keep your head down Fritzy boy,
Last night in the pale moonlight
We saw you – we saw you.

You were mending your broken wire
And we opened rapid fire.
If you want to see your mother
And your fatherland,
Keep your head down Fritzy boy.

Hold your hands up Fritzy boy,
Hold your hands up Fritzy boy,
Just tonight in the pale moonlight
We saw you – we saw you.
We were laying some more wire
And we nearly opened fire.
If you want to see your mother
And your fatherland,
Keep your hands up Fritzy boy.

Keep your head down, Fusilier,
Keep your head down, Fusilier,
There's a bloody great Hun,
With a bloody great gun,
Who'll shoot you – who'll shoot you.
There's a sniper up a tree,
He's waiting for you and me.
If you really want to see
Ole' Blighty once more,
Keep your head down Fusilier.

'It's A Long Way To Tipperary', 1912

Music and lyrics: Jack Judge

Written for a 5-shilling bet between Judge and a friend who said he couldn't compose and perform a new song by the next day. The idea came to Judge as he travelled home on the bus, where he heard someone say 'It's a long way to…' He went home and wrote the lyrics, using Tipperary simply because it sounded right. It was first sung by the Connaught Rangers as they marched through Boulogne on 13 August 1914 and was soon adopted by most of the British Army.

Up to mighty London
Came an Irishman one day.
As the streets are paved with gold,
Sure, everyone was gay,
Singing songs of Piccadilly,
Strand and Leicester Square,
Till Paddy got excited,
Then he shouted to them there:

CHORUS:
It's a long way to Tipperary,
It's a long way to go.
It's a long way to Tipperary,
To the sweetest girl I know!
Goodbye, Piccadilly,
Farewell, Leicester Square!
It's a long, long way to Tipperary,
But my heart's right there.

Paddy wrote a letter,
To his Irish Molly-O,
Saying, 'Should you not receive it,
Write and let me know!'
'If I make mistakes in spelling,
Molly, dear,' said he,
'Remember, it's the pen that's bad,
Don't lay the blame on *me!*'

REPEAT CHORUS.

Molly wrote a neat reply,
To Irish Paddy-O,
Saying 'Mike Maloney
Wants to marry me, and so,
Leave the Strand and Piccadilly,
Or you'll be to blame,
For love has fairly drove me silly:
Hoping you're the same!'

REPEAT CHORUS.

Patriotic Records

Mr. STEWART GARDNER
10-inch Records, 3s. 6d.

4-2493	One United Front	*Bradwell*
4-2498	Sons of Old Britannia	*Forster*
4-2492	Little Mother	*Buchanan*
4-2497	Sons of the Motherland	*Monckton*
4-2496	The Soldiers of the King	*Stuart*
4-2495	Private Tommy Atkins	*Potter*

12-inch Record, 5s. 6d.

02548	England! Thy Name!	*Lewis Barnes**

(*Composer of The King's Command March coupled with Trot of the Cavalry, by Coldstream Guards Band, No. B222, 10-inch, 3/6).

DESCRIPTIVE RECORD
10-inch Record, 3s. 6d.

9473 British Troops passing through Boulogne

12-inch Record, 5s. 6d.

C 377 { A Drill Sergeant
Words of Command
A Signalling Sergeant-Instructor
Morse Code—Alphabet and Message

METROPOLITAN MILITARY BAND
12-inch Records, 5s. 6d.

C 378 { "Allies in Arms." Selection I.*
"Allies in Arms." Selection II.†

*Selection I. contains Opening, "Hearts of Oak (England), "La Brabanconne" (Belgium), "St. Patrick" (Ireland), "Russian Hymn" (Russia), "Rule Britannia" (England), "See the Conquering Hero" (England). Finale.

†Selection II. contains "La Marseillaise" (France), "The Garb of Old Gaul" (Scotland), "The Maple Leaf" (Canada), "Marcia Reale" (Italy), "Men of Harlech" (Wales), "God Save the King" (England).

C 379 { Salut à Liège (dedicated to the Brave Belgians) *Entwistle*
United Forces March

C 380 { "Our Sailor King," Patriotic March *Gay*
"Fighting for Liberty," Patriotic March *Kaye*

BUGLERS OF H.M. COLDSTREAM GUARDS
10-inch Record, 3s. 6d.

B 261 { Regimental Calls, No. 1
" " " 2

B 262 { Camp Calls, No. 1
" " " 2

(Author's collection)

'That's The Wrong Way To Tickle Mary'

A parody on the tune: 'It's A Long Way To Tipperary'

The reference to moustaches in the second verse was as a result of the War Office reversing its policy in 1916 on soldiers being permitted to have facial hair, which by then was regarded as unsanitary and potentially dangerous in the case of facial wounds. Officers were still permitted to have them, but many removed theirs as they became an easy target for German snipers.

That's the wrong way to tickle Mary
That's the wrong way to kiss,
Don't you know that over here lad,
They like it better like this.
Hooray pour la France,
Farewell Angleterre,
We didn't know how to tickle Mary,
But now we've learnt how.

It took a long time to get it hairy,
T'was a long time to grow,
It took a long time to get it hairy,
For the tooth-brush hairs to show.
Good bye Charlie Chaplin,
Farewell tufts of hair,
T'was a long, long time to get it hairy,
Now my upper lip's quite bare.

The following two songs were some of the dozens of popular tunes imported from the United States. Many found their way across the Atlantic as show tunes, but most were simply purchased as sheet music, where they found a ready audience in England. Their simple 'moon, June, tune' lyrics, and heavily sentimental messages made them perennial hits with the soldiers, notwithstanding the fact that most had little idea, if any, where Tennessee or Texas actually was.

'Way Down In Tennessee', *c.* 1912

Music and lyrics: George L. Cobb.

Cobb was a prolific ragtime composer, but this unusually homely song appealed to the sentimentality of the British soldiers, who would often sing it quietly and in a slightly mournful way.

Way down in Tennessee,
That's where I long to be.
Right at my mother's knee,
She thinks the world of me.
All I can think of tonight
Is the fields of snowy white, banjos ringing, darkies singing,
All the world seems bright.
The rose round the door
Make me love you more.
I'll see my sweetheart Flo,
And the friends I used to know.
They'll be right there to meet me,

Just imagine how they'll greet me,

When I get back,

When I get back,

To my home in Tennessee.

'Down Texas Way', 1912

Music and lyrics: Unknown

This is very much in the genre of the former song, with a heavy bias towards home and parents, but, typically of the British soldiers, it was frequently modified to 'Down Wipers Way'.

Down Texas Way,

'Mid the clover and the new-mown hay,

Where they'll be so glad,

Yes so glad,

To see me-eee.

Night and day,

I can see their happy faces gay,

And hear a sweet voice say,

'Come along there,

To a beauty little, cutie little

Spot down yonder.'

Let me play,

'Mid the clover again at dear old mother's knee,

I long to kneel and pray,

God bless mother,

God bless dad,

Make them happy

Make them glad,

I'm in heaven,

Down old Texas way.

'Danny Boy', 1913

Tune: 'Londonderry Air'
Music and lyrics: Frederick Weatherley

Weatherley was remarkable in writing two of the most popular tunes of the early 20th century, 'Danny Boy' and 'Roses Of Picardy'. The exact meaning of the lyrics is disputed; most likely it was a message from a parent to a son leaving for war, but many believe it to have been a reference to the Irish troubles that plagued politics at the time.

Oh, Danny boy, the pipes, the pipes are calling,

From glen to glen, and down the mountain side,

The summer's gone, and all the flow'rs are dying,

'Tis you, 'tis you must go and I must bide.

But come ye back when summer's in the meadow,

Or when the valley's hushed and white with snow,

'Tis I'll be here in sunshine or in shadow,

Oh, Danny boy, oh, Danny boy, I love you so.

And if you come, and all the flow'rs are dying,

If I am dead, as dead I well may be,

I pray you'll find the place where I am lying,

And kneel and say an 'Ave' there for me.

And I shall hear, though soft you tread above me,

And all my grave will warm and sweeter be,

And then you'll kneel and whisper that you love me,
And I shall sleep in peace until you come to me.

'Who Were You With Last Night?' 1913

Music and lyrics: Mark Sheridan

Sheridan's real name was Frederick Shaw, who was a popular pre-war music hall artist and prolific songwriter. He also wrote the extremely clever 1914 patriotic song 'Belgium Put The Kibosh On The Kaiser'.

Who were you with last night?
Who were you with last night?
It wasn't your sister.
It wasn't your ma.
Ah! ah! ah! ah! ah! ah! ah! ah!
Who were you with last night,
Out in the pale moonlight?
Are you going to tell your Missus
When you get home,
Who were you with last night?

Who were you with last night?
Who were you squeezing so tight?
It wasn't your sister.
It wasn't your ma.
Ah! ah! ah! ah! ah! ah! ah! ah!
Who were you with last night,
Out in the pale moonlight?
I am going to tell your missus

When you get home,
Just who you were with last night!
I am going to tell your missus
When you get home,
Just who you were with last night!

'Who Stole The Rum Last Night?'

A parody of the tune: 'Who Were You With Last Night?'

Who stole the rum last night?
Who stole the rum last night?
Was it the sergeant who lifted the jar?
Ah ha ha ha ha ha ha ha ha.

Who stole the rum last night?
Out in the pale moonlight?
I'm going to tell the colonel
When I get back that –
You stole the rum last night.

'There's A Long, Long Trail', 1913

Music: Zo Elliott. Lyrics: Stoddart King

Without a doubt the most widely sung of all American
songs, it was a clever song that invoked the homesickness
all soldiers felt. It was frequently used as the final song
at concerts for the troops and was usually followed by a
very long silence.

Nights are growing very lonely,
Days are very long;
I'm a-growing weary only
List'ning for your song.
Old remembrances are thronging,
Thro' my memory,
Till it seems the world is full of dreams,
Just to call you back to me.

There's a long, long trail a-winding,
Into the land of my dreams,
Where the nightingales are singing,
And a white moon beams.
There's a long, long night of waiting,
Until my dreams all come true;
Till the day when I'll be going down
That long, long trail with you.
All night long I hear you calling,
Calling sweet and low;
I seem to hear your footsteps falling,
Ev'rywhere I go.
Tho' the road between us stretches
Many a weary mile,
I forget that you're not with me yet,
When I think I see you smile.

There's a long, long trail a-winding,
Into the land of my dreams,
Where the nightingales are singing,
And a white moon beams.
There's a long, long night of waiting,
Until my dreams all come true;

Till the day when I'll be going down
That long, long trail with you.

'Hello, Hello, Who's Your Lady Friend?' 1913

Music: Harry Fragson.
Lyrics: Worton David and Bert Lee

Fragson was an early superstar of the music halls, a witty performer and millionaire who was feted by the elite of Paris, where he lived. This song was a huge hit on both sides of the channel, but alas it did him little good. He was shot dead by his demented father in early 1913.

Jeremiah Jones a ladies' man was he.
Ev'ry pretty girl he loved to spoon:
Till he found a wife,
And down beside the sea,
Went to Margate for the honeymoon;
But when he strolled along the promenade
With his little wife, just newly wed,
He got an awful scare,
When someone strolling there,
Come up to him and winked and said:

CHORUS:
Hello! Hello! Who's your lady friend?
Who's the little girlie by your side?
I've seen you with a girl or two.
Oh! Oh! Oh! I am surprised at you;
Hello! Hello! Stop your little games.

241

Don't you think your ways
You ought to mend?
It isn't the girl I saw you with at Uvongo
Who? Who? Who's your lady friend?

Jeremiah took his wife's mama one night;
Round to see a moving picture show.
There upon the screen,
A picture came in sight
Jeremiah cried, he'd better go.
For on that picture there was Jeremiah
With a pretty girl upon his knee.
Ma cried, 'What does it mean?'
Then pointing to the screen.
The people yelled at Jones with glee:

REPEAT CHORUS.

'Colonel Bogey', 1914

Music: F.J. Ricketts

Although most people believe it to be inspired by the Second World War, it was composed by Lieutenant F.J. Ricketts in 1914. Ricketts went on to become bandmaster for the Royal Marines. It was never set to words, but as a tune, it was the first to sell over a million copies of sheet music. The name was actually based on the 'Bogey' scoring system in golf. It was adopted during the war as the marching tune of the 10th and 50th battalions, Canadian Expeditionary Force.

'Sister Susie's Sewing Shirts For Soldiers', 1914

Music: Herman Darewski. Lyrics: R.P. Weston

An American song that was performed widely, one of its more notable vocalists being Al Jolson, who recorded his version of the song in 1916. Each verse was supposed to be sung faster than the previous one, often difficult for soldiers when quantities of beer had been consumed. There was another version, which was possibly the only song ever dedicated to the snipers of the Great War. (See Appendix 7.)

Sister Susie's sewing in the kitchen on a 'Singer'.
There's miles and miles of flannel on the floor and up the stairs,
And father says it's rotten getting mixed up with the cotton,
And sitting on the needles that she leaves upon the chairs.
And should you knock at our street door, Ma whispers,
'Come inside.'
Then when you ask where Susie is, she says with loving pride:

'Sister Susie's sewing shirts for soldiers,
Such skill at sewing shirts
Our shy young sister Susie shows!
Some soldiers send epistles,
Say they'd sooner sleep in thistles
Than the saucy, soft, short shirts for soldiers sister Susie sews.'

Piles and piles and piles of shirts she sends out to the soldiers,
And sailors won't be jealous when they see them, not at all.
And when we say her stitching will set all the soldiers itching,
She says our soldiers fight best when their back's against the wall.

And little brother Gussie, he who lisps when he says 'yes',
Says 'Where's the cotton gone from off my kite? Oh, I can gueth!'

(faster)
'Sister Susie's sewing shirts for soldiers,
Such skill at sewing shirts
Our shy young sister Susie shows!
Some soldiers send epistles,
Say they'd sooner sleep in thistles
Than the saucy, soft, short shirts for soldiers sister Susie sews.'

I forgot to tell you that our sister Susie's married,
And when she isn't sewing shirts, she's sewing other things.
Then little sister Molly says, 'Oh, sister's bought a dolly.
She's making all the clothes for it with pretty bows and strings.'
Says Susie: 'Don't be silly,' as she blushes and she sighs.
Then mother smiles and whispers, with a twinkle in her eyes:

'Sister Susie's sewing shirts for soldiers,
Such skill at sewing shirts
Our shy young sister Susie shows!
Some soldiers send epistles,
Say they'd sooner sleep in thistles
Than the saucy, soft, short shirts for soldiers sister Susie sews.'

'Sister Susie's sewing shirts for soldiers,
Such skill at sewing shirts
Our shy young sister Susie shows!
Some soldiers send epistles,
Say they'd sooner sleep in thistles
Than the saucy, soft, short shirts for soldiers sister Susie sews.'

'Belgium Put The Kibosh On The Kaiser', 1914

Music and lyrics: Mark Sheridan

A clever song that poked fun at the Kaiser and his allies, written just after the BEF and Belgian armies had managed, by fierce defence, to stop the advancing German Army. It was much performed in music halls in 1914 and early 1915, but gradually fell out of favour as the war dragged on.

A silly German sausage
Dreamt Napoleon he'd be,
Then he went and broke his promise,
It was made in Germany.
He shook hands with Britannia,
And eternal peace he swore,
Naughty boy, he talked of peace,
While he prepared for war.

He stirred up little Serbia
To serve his dirty tricks,
But naughty nights at Liege
Quite upset this Dirty Dick.
His luggage labelled 'England',
And his programme nicely set,
He shouted 'First stop Paris',
But he hasn't got there yet.

CHORUS:
For Belgium put the kibosh the Kaiser,
Europe took the stick and made him sore;

On his throne it hurts to sit,
And when John Bull starts to hit,
He will never sit upon it any more.

His warships sailed upon the sea,
They looked a pretty sight,
But when they heard the bulldog bark,
They disappeared from sight.
The Kaiser said 'Be careful,
If by Jellicoe they're seen,
Then every man-of-war I've got
Will be a submarine.'

We chased his ship to Turkey,
And the Kaiser startled stood,
Scratch'd his head and said 'Don't hurt,
You see I'm touching wood';
Then Turkey brought her warships
Just to aid the German plot,
Be careful, Mr Turkey,
Or you'll do the Turkey Trot.

REPEAT CHORUS.

He'll have to go to school again,
And learn his geography,
He quite forgot Britannia,
And the hands across the sea;
Australia and Canada,
the Russian and the Jap,
And England looked so small
He couldn't see her on the map.

Whilst Ireland seemed unsettled,
'Ah,' said he 'I'll settle John',
But he didn't know the Irish
Like he knew them later on.
Though the Kaiser stirred the lion,
Please excuse him for the crime,
His lunatic attendant
Wasn't with him at the time.

REPEAT CHORUS.

DOING THEIR BIT.

(Punch)

'Keep The Home Fires Burning', 1914

Music: Ivor Novello. Lyrics: Lena Ford

Originally published as 'Till The Boys Come Home' it was re-published in 1915 under its new title. It paralleled 'Tipperary' in popularity in England but unlike the former, it retained its popularity throughout the conflict, partly because of its hopeful sentiment – everyone wanted their loved ones to come home. Novello was to become Britain's greatest show songwriter of the 20th century and the Ivor Novello Award is still presented annually to Britain's most outstanding composers and songwriters. Ironically, Lena Ford was killed in the last air raid on London in March 1918.

They were summoned from the hillside,
They were called in from the glen,
And the country found them ready
At the stirring call for men.
Let no tears add to their hardships,
As the soldiers pass along,
And although your heart is breaking,
Make it sing this cheery song:
Keep the Home Fires Burning,
While your hearts are yearning.
Though your lads are far away,
They dream of home.
There's a silver lining,
Through the dark clouds shining,
Turn the dark cloud inside out,
Till the boys come home.

Overseas there came a pleading,
'Help a nation in distress',
And we gave our glorious laddies –
Honour bade us do no less,
For no gallant son of Britain
To a tyrant's yoke shall bend,
And no Englishman is silent
To the sacred call of 'Friend'.
Keep the Home Fires Burning,
While your hearts are yearning.
Though your lads are far away,
They dream of home.
There's a silver lining,
Through the dark clouds shining,
Turn the dark cloud inside out,
Till the boys come home.

'They Didn't Believe Me', 1914

Music: Jerome Kern. Lyrics: Herbert Reynolds

The first of Kern's many successes, it also provided the basis for the haunting parody 'And When They Ask Us'.

Got the cutest little way,
Like to watch you all the day,
And it certainly seems fine,
Just to think that you'll be mine.

When I see your pretty smile,
Makes the living worth the while,

So I've got to run around,
Telling people what I've found.

And when I told them how beautiful you are
They didn't believe me! They didn't believe me!
Your lips, your eyes, your cheeks, your hair,
Are in a class beyond compare,
You're the loveliest girl that one could see!

And when I tell them,
And I cert'nly am goin' to tell them,
That I'm the man whose wife one day you'll be,
They'll never believe me,
They'll never believe me,
That from this great big world you've chosen me!

Don't know how it happen'd quite,
May have been the summer night,
May have been, well, who can say!
Things just happen any way.

All I know is I said 'Yes!'
Hesitating more or less,
And you kissed me where I stood,
Just like any fellow would.

And when I told them how wonderful you are
They didn't believe me! They didn't believe me!
Your lips, your eyes, your curly hair
Are in a class beyond compare
You're the loveliest thing that one could see!

And when I tell them,
And I cert'nly am goin' to tell them,
That I'm the girl whose boy one day you'll be,
They'll never believe me,
They'll never believe me,
That from this great big world you've chosen me!

'And When They Ask Us'

A parody of the tune: 'They Didn't Believe Me'

And when they ask us how dangerous it was,
Oh! we'll never tell them. No we'll never tell them.
We spent each day in some café,
And chatted French girls night and day;
It was the cushiest job we ever had.
And when they ask us,
And they're certainly going to ask us,
The reason why we didn't win the Croix de Guerre,
Oh! we'll never tell them, no we'll never tell them,
There was a front – but damned if we knew where.

'I'll Make A Man Of You', 1914

*Music and lyrics: Arthur Wimperis and
Herman Fink*

One of the best known recruiting songs of the early war period, it was performed thousands of times in venues up and down the country. The cast was usually joined by a recruiting sergeant and sometimes a regimental band, and the rousing music often persuaded the faint of heart to enlist. It was beautifully shown in the film version of *Oh What A Lovely War*.

The Army and the Navy need attention,
The outlook isn't healthy you'll admit,
But I've got a perfect dream of a new recruiting scheme,

Near-sighted Old Lady (a keen recruiter). "Now look at that young fellow. A couple of months in the army would make a new man of him!" (Punch)

Which I think is absolutely it.
If only other girls would do as I do,
I believe that we could manage it alone,
For I turn all suitors from me but the sailor and the Tommy,
I've an army and a navy of my own.

On Sunday I walk out with a Soldier,
On Monday I'm taken by a Tar,
On Tuesday I'm out with a baby Boy Scout,
On Wednesday a Hussar;
On Thursday a gang oot wi' a Scottie,
On Friday, the Captain of the crew;
But on Saturday I'm willing, if you'll only take the shilling,
To make a man of any one of you.

I teach the tenderfoot to face the powder,
That gives an added lustre to my skin,
And I show the raw recruit how to give a chaste salute,
So when I'm presenting arms he's falling in.
It makes you almost proud to be a woman.
When you make a strapping soldier of a kid.
And he says 'You put me through it and I didn't want to do it
But you went and made me love you so I did.'

On Sunday I walk out with a Bo'sun.
On Monday a Rifleman in green,
On Tuesday I choose a 'sub' in the 'Blues',
On Wednesday a Marine;
On Thursday a Terrier from Tooting,
On Friday a Midshipman or two,
But on Saturday I'm willing, if you'll only take the shilling,
To make a man of any one of you.

'Your King And Country Want You', 1914

Tune: 'We Don't Want To Lose You'
Music and lyrics: Paul Rubens

This was written as a 'women's recruitment song' and was sung in the early months of the war to encourage enlistment. The last verse had alternative lyrics for mixed audiences. It had fallen out of favour by the end of 1915. The money raised from the sale of the sheet music was donated to the Queen Mary 'Work For Women' fund, for whom it raised over half a million pounds.

We've watched you playing cricket and every kind of game
At football, golf and polo, you men have made your name,
But now your country calls you to play your part in war,
And no matter what befalls you, we shall love you all the more,
So come and join the forces as your fathers did before.

CHORUS:
Oh! we don't want to lose you but we think you ought to go,
For your King and Country both need you so;
We shall want you and miss you but with all our might and main,
We shall cheer you, thank you, kiss (bless) you,
When you come back again.

We want you from all quarters so, help us, south and north,
We want you in your thousands, from Falmouth to the Forth,
You'll never find us fail you,
When you are in distress,
So, answer when we hail you, and let your word be 'Yes'
And so your name, in years to come each mother's son shall bless.

REPEAT CHORUS.

It's easy for us women (people) to stay at home and shout,
But remember there's a duty to the men who *first* went out.
The odds against that handful were nearly four to one,
And we cannot rest until it's man for man, and gun for gun!
And every woman's (body's) duty is to see that duty done!

REPEAT CHORUS.

'Gilbert The Filbert', 1914

*Music and lyrics: Arthur Wimperis and
Herman Fink*

This became the theme song of music hall star Basil
Hallam, who was at the height of his fame when war
broke out. He insisted on enlisting in the Royal Flying
Corps, and was tragically killed at Couin on 20 August
1916, when his parachute became entangled as he tried
to escape from a drifting observation balloon.

I am known round town as a fearful blood,
For I come straight down from the dear old flood,
And I know who's who, and I know what's what,
And between the two I'm a trifle hot,
For I set the tone as you may suppose,
For I stand alone when it comes to clothes,
And as for gals just ask my pals,
Why everybody knows.

CHORUS:

I'm Gilbert the Filbert, the Knut with a K,
The pride of Piccadilly, the blasé roué.
Oh Hades, the ladies, who leave their wooden huts,
For Gilbert the Filbert, the Colonel of the Knuts.

You may look upon me as a waster, what?
But you ought to see how I fag and swot,
For I'm called by two, and by five I'm out,
Which I couldn't do if I slacked about,
Then I count my ties and I change my kit,
And the exercise keeps me awfully fit.
Once I begin I work like sin,
I'm full of go and grit.

REPEAT CHORUS.

'Burlington Bertie', 1915

Music and lyrics: W. Hargreaves

This was the story of a 'toff' who had fallen on hard times. It was first sung at Birkenhead in 1914 by American Ella Shields, the wife of the composer. Uniquely, she performed her entire act dressed in a man's dinner suit. It was oddly popular in the trenches, possibly because of the ludicrous analogy between the immaculate Bertie and the less-than-immaculate soldiers. It became something of an anthem for the working class man.

I'm Bert. P'raps you've heard of me.
Bert – You've had word of me.
Plodding along, hearty and strong,
Living on plates of fresh air.
I dress up in fashion, stick my best hat on,
and saunter along like a toff.
I walk down the Strand, my gloves on my hand,
Then I walk down again with them off.
I'm all airs and graces, correct easy paces,
Without food so long, I've forgot where my face is.
I'm Bert, Bert, I haven't a shirt,
But my people are well off, you know.
Nearly everyone knows me, from Smith to Lord Roseberry,
I'm Burlington Bertie from Bow.

I'm Burlington Bertie, I rise at ten thirty,
And Buckingham Palace I view.
I stand in the yard while they're changing the guard,
And the queen shouts across 'Toodle oo'!
The Prince of Wales' brother, along with some other,
Slaps me on the back and says, 'Come and see Mother.'
I'm Bert, Bert, and royalty's hurt,
When they ask me to dine, I say no.
I've just had a banana with Lady Diana,
I'm Burlington Bertie from Bow.

I stroll with Lord Hurlington
Roll into the Burlington,
Call for Champagne, then I walk out again,
Then I come back and I borrow the ink.
I'm Burlington Bertie, I rise at ten thirty,

And saunter along Temple Bar.

As round there I skip, I keep shouting 'Pip Pip!'

And the darn'd fools think I'm in my car.

At Rothschild's I swank it, My body I plank it,

On his front door step with *The Mail* for a blanket.

I'm Bert, Bert, and Rothschild was hurt ,

He said, 'You can't sleep there', I said, 'Oh'.

He said 'I'm Rothschild, sonny!' I said 'That's damn'd funny,

I'm Burlington Bertie from Bow.'

I smile condescendingly,

While they're extending me,

Cheer upon cheer, when I appear

Captain with my polo team.

And reach Kempton Park around three

I stand by the rail, when a horse is for sale

And there's no doubt that I'd buy one, a cert.

But where would I keep it you know?

I can't let my man see me,

In bed with a gee-gee,

I'm Burlington Bertie from Bow!

'Good Bye-ee', 1915

Music: R.P. Weston. Lyrics: Bert Lee

The idea for this song came from Weston and Lee hearing
a crowd of factory girls shouting 'Good by-ee' in a comic
manner, as a regiment of soldiers marched past. It
cleverly incorporated much of the popular officers' slang
of the war and it became a great hit in variety theatres.

Weston and Lee worked closely together to create several other songs, particularly 'Lloyd George's Beer' also reproduced below.

Brother Bertie went away,

To do his bit the other day,

With a smile on his lips,

And his Lieutenant's pips,

Upon his shoulder bright and gay.

As the train moved out he said,

'Remember me to all the birds.'

Then he wagged his paw,

And went away to war,

Shouting out these pathetic words:

CHORUS:

Goodbye-ee, goodbye-ee,

Wipe the tear, baby dear, from your eye-ee.

Tho' it's hard to part I know,

I'll be tickled to death to go.

Don't cry-ee, don't sigh-ee,

There's a silver lining in the sky-ee,

Bonsoir, old thing, cheer-i-o, chin, chin,

Nah-poo, toodle-oo, goodbye-ee.

Marmaduke Horatio Flynn

(Though he'd whiskers on his chin),

In a play took his part

And he touched every heart,

As Little Willie from East Lynne.

As the dying child he lay,

Upon his snow-white counterpane,

And amid all their tears,

All the audience gave cheers,
As he said, as he passed away:

REPEAT CHORUS.

At a concert down in Kew,
The convalescents, dressed in blue,
Had to hear Lady Lee,
Who had turned 83,
Sing all the old, old songs she knew.
Then she made a speech and said,
I look on you boys with pride,
And for all that you've done,
I'm going to kiss every one',
Then they all grabbed their sticks and cried:

REPEAT CHORUS.

Little Private Patrick Shaw,
He was a prisoner of war,
Till a hun with a gun
Called him 'Schweinhund' for fun,
And Paddy punched him on the jaw.
Across the barbed wire fence he fell
And Paddy sprinted off like hell,
And all other men could hear,
As Paddy reached the Dutch frontier,
Were the words of this song so they all sang along:

REPEAT CHORUS.

'Lloyd George's Beer Song', 1915

Music and lyrics: R.P. Weston and Bert Lee

This was a tongue-in-cheek reaction to Lloyd George's decision to cut alcohol consumption during the war by limiting licensing hours and reducing the strength of beers. Excessive drinking was the primary cause of poor levels of industrial production and factory accidents. Lloyd George's decision was naturally highly unpopular but actually proved very successful; alcohol consumption was reduced by 50 per cent and industrial production rose by almost 40 per cent.

We shall win the war, we shall win the war,
As I said before, we shall win the war.
The Kaiser's in a dreadful fury,
Now he knows we're making it at every brewery.
Have you read of it, seen what's said of it,
In the Mirror and the Mail.
It's a substitute, and a pubstitute,
And it's known as Government Ale (or otherwise).

Lloyd George's Beer, Lloyd George's Beer.
At the brewery, there's nothing doing,
All the water works are brewing,
Lloyd George's Beer, it isn't dear.
Oh they say it's a terrible war, oh law,
And there never was a war like this before,
But the worst thing that ever happened in this war
Is Lloyd George's Beer.

Buy a lot of it, all they've got of it.

Dip your bread in it, shove your head in it

From January to October,

And I'll bet a penny that you'll still be sober.

Get your cloth in it, make some broth in it,

With a pair of mutton chops.

Drown your dogs in it, pop your clogs in it,

And you'll see some wonderful sights (in that lovely stuffo).

Lloyd George's Beer, Lloyd George's Beer.

At the brewery, there's nothing doing,

All the water works are brewing,

Lloyd George's Beer, it isn't dear.

With Haig and Joffre when affairs look black,

And you can't get at Jerry with his gas attack.

Just get your squirters out and we'll squirt the buggers back,

With Lloyd George's Beer.

'Pack Up Your Troubles', 1915

*Music: Felix Powell. Lyrics: George Henry Powell
(under the pseudonym George Asaf)*

Originally written for the music hall, the tune was initially rejected by Felix Powell but rescued from his waste-bin by his brother George, who wrote the words in ten minutes. It has become one of the most evocative of all Great War songs, and was sung in music halls and in estaminets across France and Flanders and on the march.

Private Perks is a funny little codger,
With a smile, a funny smile.
Five feet none, he's an artful little dodger,
With a smile, a funny smile.
Flush or broke he'll have his little joke,
He can't be suppress'd.
All the other fellows have to grin,
When he gets this off his chest, Hi!

CHORUS:
Pack up your troubles in your old kit-bag,
And smile, smile, smile,
While you've a lucifer to light your fag,
Smile, boys, that's the style.
What's the use of worrying?
It never was worth while, so
Pack up your troubles in your old kit-bag,
And smile, smile, smile.

Private Perks went a-marching into Flanders,
With his smile, his funny smile.
He was lov'd by the privates and commanders,
For his smile, his funny smile.
When a throng of Bosches came along,
With a mighty swing,
Perks yell'd out, 'This little bunch is mine!
Keep your heads down, boys and sing,' Hi!

REPEAT CHORUS.

Private Perks he came back from Bosche-shooting
With his smile, his funny smile.
Round his home he then set about recruiting
With his smile, his funny smile.
He told all his pals, the short, the tall,
What a time he'd had;
And as each enlisted like a man
Private Perks said 'Now my lad,' Hi!

REPEAT CHORUS.

'I Didn't Raise My Boy To Be A Soldier', 1915

Music: Al Piantadosi. Lyrics: Alfred Bryan

An American work that was unusual in being one of the first anti-war songs, it was much lauded by anti-British groups in the United States – Irish, German and church ministers of many denominations. President Truman disliked it intensely, and untactfully suggested that the place for women who opposed the war was in a harem, but not the United States!

Fond Mother. "Well, good-bye, my dear boy. Take good care of yourself; and, whatever you do, always avoid trenches with a North-East aspect." (Punch)

Ten million soldiers to the war have gone,
Who may never return again.
Ten million mothers' hearts must break,
For the ones who died in vain.
Head bowed down in sorrow, in her lonely years,
I heard a mother murmur thro' her tears:

CHORUS:
I didn't raise my boy to be a soldier,
I brought him up to be my pride and joy.
Who dares to put a rifle on his shoulder,
To shoot some other mother's darling boy?
Let nations arbitrate their future troubles,
It's time to lay the sword and gun away,
There'd be no war today,
If mothers all would say:
I didn't raise my boy to be a soldier.

What victory can cheer a mother's heart,
When she looks at her blighted home?
What victory can bring her back,
All she cared to call her own?
Let each mother answer in the years to be,
Remember that my boy belongs to me!

REPEAT CHORUS.

'Jerusalem', 1916

Music: Sir Hubert Parry. Lyrics: William Blake.

At first glance, this may seem out of place with the popular songs repeated here, but the song 'Jerusalem' only dates from March 1916, when William Blake's poem was set to music by Sir Hubert Parry. The poem, which was published in 1808, was revived in 1916 by the poet laureate Robert Bridges, to boost morale and aid the 'Fight For Right' campaign. Initially, Parry was reluctant to do it and Bridges was going to ask George Butterworth instead. Ironically, he was killed on the Somme on 5 August 1916. In 1926 the song was adopted as the anthem for the National Union of Women's Suffrage Societies.

And did those feet in ancient time.
Walk upon England's mountains green:
And was the holy Lamb of God,
On England's pleasant pastures seen?

And did the Countenance Divine,
Shine forth upon our clouded hills?
And was Jerusalem builded here,
Among these dark Satanic mills?

Bring me my bow of burning gold;
Bring me my arrows of desire:
Bring me my spear: O clouds unfold!
Bring me my chariot of fire!

I will not cease from mental fight,
Nor shall my sword sleep in my hand,
'Til we have built Jerusalem,
In England's green and pleasant land.

'Take Me Back To Dear Old Blighty', 1916

*Music: Arthur J. Mills. Lyrics: Fred Godfrey and
Bennett Scott*

This was a noisy and much loved music-hall song, usually sung with gusto by soldiers at home on leave. Although it was seldom used as a marching song, the chorus was often sung in isolation, and in tough times could be heard sung softly but with great feeling from dug-outs, funk holes or during a forced march.

Jack Dunn, son of a gun, over in France today,
Keeps fit doing his bit up to his eyes in clay.
Each night after a fight to pass the time along,
He's got a little gramophone that plays this song:

CHORUS:
Take me back to dear old Blighty!
Put me on the train for London town!
Take me over there,
Drop me ANYWHERE,
Liverpool, Leeds, or Birmingham, well, I don't care!
I should love to see my best girl,
Cuddling up again we soon should be,
WHOA!!! Tiddley iddley ighty,

Hurry me home to Blighty,
Blighty is the place for me!

Bill Spry, started to fly, up in an aeroplane,
In France, taking a chance, wish'd he was down again.
Poor Bill, feeling so ill, yell'd out to Pilot Brown:
'Steady a bit, yer fool! we're turning upside down!'

REPEAT CHORUS.

Jack Lee, having his tea, says to his pal MacFayne,
'Look, chum, apple and plum! it's apple and plum again!
Same stuff, isn't it rough? fed up with it I am!
Oh! for a pot of Aunt Eliza's raspb'ry jam!'

REPEAT CHORUS.

One day Mickey O'Shea stood in a trench somewhere,
So brave, having a shave, and trying to part his hair.
Mick yells, dodging the shells and lumps of dynamite:
Talk of the Crystal Palace on a firework night!

REPEAT CHORUS.

'If You Were The Only Girl In The World', 1916

Music: Nat Ayer. Lyrics: Clifford Grey

A gentle, lilting melody that has stood the test of time, and become a standard, recorded by dozens of artists. It was first played on 19 April 1916 at the Alhambra Theatre in Leicester Square as part of the stage show *The Bing Boys Are Here* (advertised as 'A picture of London life') which itself became one of the most successful wartime revues.

Sometimes when I feel bad,

and things look blue,

I wish a pal I had … say one like you.

Someone within my heart to build a throne,

Someone who'd never part, to call my own.

If you were the only girl in the world,

and I were the only boy,

Nothing else would matter in the world today,

We could go on loving in the same old way.

A garden of Eden just made for two,

With nothing to mar our joy.

I would say such wonderful things to you,

There would be such wonderful things to do,

If you were the only girl in the world,

and I were the only boy.

'If You Were The Only Boche In The Trench

A parody on the tune:
'If You Were The Only Girl In The World'

If you were the only Boche in the trench,

And I had the only bomb;

Nothing else would matter

In the world that day,

I would blow you up into eternity.

A chamber of horrors,

Just made for two,

With nothing to spoil our fun.

There would be such

Wonderful things to do;

I should get your rifle

And bayonet too,

If you were the only

Boche in the trench

And I had the only bomb.

'Oh, How I Hate To Get Up In The Morning', 1916

Music and lyrics: Irving Berlin

Composed when Berlin was a soldier serving in the US 77th Division in 1917. The tune was inspired by the notes of the reveille played on the trumpet every morning and it became an internationally popular song. Berlin went on to become one of America's premier songwriters.

Oh! How I hate to get up in the morning,
Oh! How I'd love to remain in bed.
For the hardest blow of all is to hear the bugler call:
'You've got to get up, you've got to get up,
You've got to get up this morning!'
Someday I'm going to murder the bugler,
Someday they're going to find him dead.
I'll amputate his reveille and stomp upon it heavily,
And spend the rest of my life in bed!
A bugler in the army is the luckiest of men,
He wakes the boys at five and then goes back to bed again,
He doesn't have to blow again until the afternoon,
If ev'rything goes well with me I'll be a bugler soon!
Oh! How I hate to get up in the morning,
Oh! How I'd love to remain in bed.
For the hardest blow of all is to hear the bugler call:
'You've got to get up, you've got to get up,
You've got to get up this morning!'
Oh, boy! The minute the battle is over,
Oh, boy! The minute the foe is dead,
I'll put my uniform away and move to Philadelphia,
And spend the rest of my life in bed!

(Topfoto)

Young wife (at sound of explosion). "Thomas! Thomas! The Zeppelins are here! *Did you lock the front door?*" (Punch)

G.O.C. "Well, my man, what are you in civilian life?"

Dejected Private. "Professor of Greek History at one of the Universities, sir." (Punch)

The New Submarine Danger

" They'll be torpedoin' us if we stick 'ere much longer, Bill "

THE BOILING POINT.

(Punch)

(Mary Evans)

THE SINEWS OF WAR.

PRIVATE ATKINS. "FOR WHAT WE HAVE RECEIVED—AND ARE GOING TO RECEI
HERE'S TO THE A.S.C."

(Punch)

Gretel. "Have you ever contemplated what would happen to us all should the enemy triumph?"

Hansel. "Don't, Gretel — don't. Fancy being forced to play cricket!" (Punch)

(Topfoto)

DELIVERING THE GOODS.

(Punch)

THE ROSE OF
"NO MAN'S LAND".

WORDS BY J. Caddigan.

MUSIC BY JAMES A. BRENNAN.

Sung by

Dollie
AND
Billie.

Photo by

Copyright. ———— ✳ ———— *Price 6ᵈ net.*

HERMAN DAREWSKI MUSIC PUBLISHING Cº
(ST SWITHIN'S SYNDICATE LTP)
Incorporating CHAS. SHEARD & Cº
122 & 124, CHARING CROSS ROAD, LONDON, W.C. 2.
Copyright, MCMXVIII, by Leo Feist Inc. New York.
PRINTED IN ENGLAND.

(Topfoto)

That tin hat feels something like this on the way to the offensive

And about like this when you get there

My Hat!

Helmets, Shrapnel, One.

(Bruce Bairnsfather, author's collection)

Hail, Columba!
President Wilson (*to American Eagle*).
"Gee! What a dove I've made of you!"
(Punch)

Nobbled
"'ow long are you up for, Bill?"
"Seven years"
"Yer lucky—, I'm duration"
(Bruce Bairnsfather, author's collection)

The Whip Hand
Private Mulligatawny (the Australian Stock-whip wonder) frequently causes a lot of bother in
the enemy's trenches. (Bruce Bairnsfather, author's collection)

(Bruce Bairnsfather, author's collection)

'Down Where The Swanee River Flows', 1916

Music: Albert Von Tilzer.
Lyrics: Charles McCarron, Charles S. Alberte

Ironically, the composer was an ex-patriot German, living in America. The message of the song was slightly more sophisticated than many others from America, with less of the mawkish sentimentality, and the tune was extremely jolly.

I had a big surprise today,

While in a ten cent photo play,

I saw my old home town,

Way down in Dixieland.

It was simply grand, just to sit right there,

And gaze on the scenes of bygone days.

Made me yearn to return to the land,

And people I will love always.

I even saw the same old school,

Where I learned the golden rule.

I'd like to meet the movie man,

I want to shake him by the hand.

I want to tell him that he wrote a grand scenario,

He knew where to go.

Plain as day upon the screen,

Hezakiah can be seen.

Little Mose, on his toes,

Looking at the camera, nearly spoiled the scene.

I saw the cotton white as foam,
I saw my home sweet home.

Down where the Swanee River flows,
I want to be there.
Down where the cotton blossom grows,
I want to see there,
My little sister Flo',
Keepin' time with Uncle Joe,
Singing a song and raggin' on his old banjo.
I see my dear old mother
Oh, Lordy, Lordy, Lordy, how I love her.
When the birds are singing in the wildwood,
My happy childhood
Comes back once more.
My heart is sore, that's why I'm
Going back where they care for me.
Every night they say a little prayer for me,
Down where the Swanee River flows.

'The Rose Of No-Man's Land', 1916

Music: Jack Caddigan.
Lyrics: James Alexander Brennan

One of the first songs to be written about the women who served during the war, in this instance the VAD nurses. For some reason it was particularly liked by French soldiers and was translated into a French language version by Louis Delamarre.

I've seen some beautiful flowers,
Grow in life's garden fair,
I've spent some wonderful hours,
Lost in their fragrance rare;
But I have found another,
Wondrous beyond compare.

CHORUS:
There's a rose that grows on 'No-Man's Land'
And it's wonderful to see,
Tho' it's spray'd with tears, it will live for years,
In my garden of memory.
It's the one red rose the soldier knows,
It's the work of the Master's hand;
Mid the War's great curse,
Stands the Red Cross Nurse,
She's the rose of 'No-Man's Land'.

Out of the heavenly splendour,
Down to the trail of woe,
God in his mercy has sent her,
Cheering the world below;
We call her 'Rose of Heaven',
We've learned to love her so.

REPEAT CHORUS.

'Roses Of Picardy', 1916

Music: Haydn Wood.
Lyrics: F. Weatherly

Arguably the most famous and performed sentimental song of the Great War. According to Weatherly the lyrics came to him one night as he sat on a London bus, so he jumped off and scribbled the words down on an old envelope. It sold as sheet music at the rate of 50,000 per month and was extensively used to help men with shell-shock to recover their speech. It has been recorded an estimated 150 times, the last being in 2011.

She is watching by the poplars, Colinette with the sea-blue eyes,
She is watching and longing and waiting where the long white
roadway lies.
And a song stirs in the silence, as the wind in the boughs above,
She listens and starts and trembles, 'tis the first little song of love:

CHORUS:
Roses are shining in Picardy, in the hush of the silver dew,
Roses are flowering in Picardy, but there's never a rose like you!
And the roses will die with the summertime, and our roads may be
far apart,
But there's one rose that dies not in Picardy!
'Tis the rose that I keep in my heart!

And the years fly on for ever, 'til the shadows veil their skies,
But he loves to hold her little hands, and look in her sea-blue eyes.
And she sees the road by the poplars, where they met in the bygone
years,

For the first little song of the roses is the last little song she hears:

REPEAT CHORUS.

'K-K-K-K-Katy', 1917

Music and lyrics: Jeffrey O'Hara

This curious tune, advertised as 'The sensational new stammering song' was one of many available for the new gramophone players, and hundreds were brought to the front by officers who had heard it whilst on leave in England. At least one battalion commander banned it because of its repetitious playing!

Jimmy was a soldier brave and bold,
Katy was a maid with hair of gold,
Like an act of fate,
Kate was standing at the gate,
Watching all the boys on dress parade.
Jimmy with the girls was just a gawk,
Stuttered ev'ry time he tried to talk,
Still that night at eight,
He was there at Katy's gate,
Stuttering to her this love sick cry.

CHORUS:
K-K-K-Katy, beautiful Katy,
You're the only g-g-g-girl that I adore;
When the m-m-m-moon shines,
Over the cowshed,

I'll be waiting at the k-k-k-kitchen door.
K-K-K-Katy, beautiful Katy,
You're the only g-g-g-girl that I adore;
When the m-m-m-moon shines,
Over the cowshed,
I'll be waiting at the k-k-k-kitchen door.

No one ever looked so nice and neat,
No one could be just as cute and sweet,
That's what Jimmy thought,
When the wedding ring he bought,
Now he's off to France the foe to meet.
Jimmy thought he'd like to take a chance,
See if he could make the Kaiser dance,
Stepping to a tune,
All about the silv'ry moon,
This is what they hear in far off France.

REPEAT CHORUS.

'Adieu La Vie (Chanson de Craonne)', 1917

Composer: Paul Vaillant-Couturier

Few French songs were popular with the British soldiers, but this, often sung by French girls in the cafes and theatres behind the lines, had a particularly haunting chorus that even British soldiers managed to master. It was a bitter and critical tune that originated after the terrible, mis-managed fighting on the Craonne plateau in 1917. The song was banned in France until 1974, when the composer, a veteran of the Craonne fighting, was finally able to remove the original manuscript from where it had been hidden. For the translation, see Appendix 8.

Quand au bout d'huit jours le r'pos terminé,

On va reprendre les tranchées,

Notre place est si utile

Que sans nous on prend la pile.

Mais c'est bien fini, on en a assez,

Personne ne veut plus marcher.

Et le cœur bien gros, comm' dans un sanglot,

On dit adieu aux civ'lots.

Même sans tambours, même sans trompettes

On s'en va là-haut en baissant la tête.

CHORUS:

Adieu la vie, adieu l'amour,

Adieu toutes les femmes.

C'est bien fini, c'est pour toujours

De cette guerre infâme.

C'est à Craonne sur le plateau,

Qu'on doit laisser sa peau.
Car nous sommes tous condamnés,
C'est nous les sacrifiés.

Huit jours de tranchée, huit jours de souffrance,
Pourtant on a l'espérance,
Que ce soir viendra la r'lève,
Que nous attendons sans trêve
Soudain dans la nuit et le silence.
On voit quelqu'un qui s'avance,
C'est un officier de chasseurs à pied,
Qui vient pour nous remplacer.
Doucement dans l'ombre sous la pluie qui tombe,
Les petits chasseurs vont chercher leurs tombes.

REPEAT CHORUS.

C'est malheureux d'voir sur les grands boulevards,
Tous ces gros qui font la foire.
Si pour eux la vie est rose
Pour nous c'est pas la même chose.
Au lieu d'se cacher tous ces embusqués,
Feraient mieux d'monter aux tranchées.
Pour défendre leur bien, car nous n'avons rien,
Nous autres les pauv' purotins.
Tous les camarades sont enterrés là,
Pour défendr' les biens de ces messieurs là.

REPEAT CHORUS.

Ceux qu'ont le pognon, ceux-là reviendront,
Car c'est pour eux qu'on crève.

Mais c'est fini, car les trouffions
Vont tous se mettre en grève.
Ce s'ra votre tour messieurs les gros
De monter sur l'plateau.
Car si vous voulez faire la guerre,
Payez-la de votre peau.

'Me And My Gal', 1917

Music: George W. Meyer.
Lyrics: Edgar Leslie and Ray Goetz

Another of Al Jolson's early recordings, this was to become a music standard, gaining even more popularity after its use in the eponymous 1942 film starring Judy Garland and Gene Kelly.

CHORUS:
The bells are ringing for me and my gal,
The birds are singing for me and my gal.
Everybody's been knowing,
To a wedding they're going,
And for weeks they've been sewing,
Every Susie and Sal.
They're congregating for me and my gal,
The parson's waiting for me and my gal.

And sometime
I'm goin' to build a little home for two,
For three or four or more,
In Love-land for me and my gal.

See the relatives there,
Looking over the pair!
They can tell at a glance,
It's a loving romance.

It's a wonderful sight,
As the families unite.
Gee! It makes the boy proud,
As he says to the crowd:

REPEAT CHORUS.

And sometime
I'm goin' to build a little home for two,
For three or four or more,
In Love-land for me and my gal.

REPEAT CHORUS.

Romance, 1917
"Darling, every potato that I have is yours" (engaged)
(Bruce Bairnsfather, author's collection)

'Over There', 1917

Music and lyrics:
George M. Cohan

The American equivalent to Britain's 'Tipperary' or 'Keep The Home Fires Burning' the tune was the most popular song in the United States during the war. Cohan was already a great composer, having penned 'Give My Regards To Broadway' and 'I'm A Yankee Doodle Dandy' and when he read of America's declaration of war on 6 April 1917, he began to work on a tune. By the time he arrived at work that morning he had the entire song composed in his head, and it subsequently sold over two million copies.

Johnnie get your gun, get your gun, get your gun,
Take it on the run, on the run, on the run.
Hear them calling you and me,
Every son of liberty,
Hurry right away, no delay, go today.
Make your daddy glad to have had such a lad,
Tell your sweetheart not to pine,
To be proud her boy's in line.

CHORUS:
Over there, over there,
Send the word, send the word over there,
That the Yanks are coming, the Yanks are coming,
The drums are rum-tumming everywhere.
So prepare, say a prayer,
Send the word, send the word to beware,

We'll be over there, we're coming over,
And we won't come back till it's over, over there.

Johnnie get your gun, get your gun, get your gun,
Johnnie show the Hun you're a son of a gun.
Hoist the flag and let her fly,
Yankee Doodle do or die,
Pack your little kit, show your grit, do your bit,
Yankees to the ranks from the towns and the tanks,
Make your mother proud of you,
And the old Red White and Blue.

REPEAT CHORUS.

'Oh! It's A Lovely War!' 1917

Music: J.P. Long. Lyrics: M. Scott

A satirical song with great appeal, it was a favourite
with soldiers who would sing it in the streets, often to
the fury of senior officers, who could do little to prevent
it. It became the title to the greatest of all film satires on
the Great War, *Oh What A Lovely War*.

CHORUS:
Oh, oh, oh, it's a lovely war.
Who wouldn't be a soldier, eh?
Oh, it's a shame to take the pay;
As soon as reveille is gone,
We feel just as heavy as lead,
But we never get up till the sergeant

Brings us breakfast up to bed.

Oh, oh, oh, it's a lovely war.

What do we want with eggs and ham,

When we've got plum and apple jam?

Form fours, right turn,

How shall we spend the money we earn?

Oh, oh, oh, it's a lovely war.

Up to your waist in water,

Up to your eyes in slush,

Using the kind of language,

That makes the sergeant blush.

Who wouldn't join the army?

That's what we all inquire;

Don't we pity the poor civilian,

Sitting beside the fire.

REPEAT CHORUS.

'Are We Downhearted – No!' 1917

Music: Will Donaldson. Lyrics: Eric Stedman

A jolly song that appeared in the theatres in 1917, when the public were becoming war-weary. The tune echoed people's determination to see the war to its final conclusion. It was often sung by men on the march, who, after the line 'Are we downhearted?', shouted a rousing 'Yes!'

The writers since the war began have written lots of things,
About our gallant soldier lads, which no-one ever sings.
Although their words are very good, the lilt they seem to miss,
For Tommy likes a jolly song, a song that goes like this:

CHORUS:
Here we are, here we are,
Here we are again!
There's Pat and Mac and Tommy and Jack and Joe.
When there's trouble brewing,
When there's something doing,
Are we downhearted? NO, let 'em all come.
Here we are, here we are,
Here we are again!
Fit and well and feeling as right as rain.
Never mind the weather,
Now then all together,
Hullo, hullo,
Here we are again!
Are we downhearted? No, let 'em all come.
Here we are, here we are,
Here we are again!
When things are getting tight,
We'll put up such a fight,
Are we downhearted? NO, let 'em all come.

When Tommy went across the sea, to bear the battle's brunt,
Of course he sang this little song whilst marching to the front.
And when he's walking through Berlin he'll sing this anthem still,
He'll light a Woodbine up and say 'How are you Kaiser Bill?'

REPEAT CHORUS.

And when the boys have finished up with Herman and with Max,
And when the enemy's got where the chicken got the axe,
The girls will all be waiting, 'midst the cheering and the din,
To hear their sweethearts singing, as their ship comes sailing in:

REPEAT CHORUS.

'Send Me Away With A Smile', 1917

Music and lyrics: Louis Weslyn and Al Piantadosi

An American version of Britain's 'Keep The Home Fires Burning' it had all the hallmarks of the popular sentimental ballads of the period.

Little girl don't cry,
I must say goodbye.
Don't you hear the bugle call?
And the fife and drum beats all.
With the flag wave o'er us all.
Tho' I love you so,
It is time to go,
And the soldier in me you'll find,
When on land or sea,
Many boys like me,
You would not have me stay behind?

CHORUS:
So, send me away with a smile, little girl,

"Old Moore" at the Front
"As far as I can make out from this 'ere prophecy-book, Bill, the seventh year is going to be the worst, and after that every fourteenth!" (Bruce Bairnsfather, author's collection)

Brush the tears from eyes of brown.
It's all for the best,
And I'm off with the rest,
With the boys from my hometown.
It may be forever we part little girl,
But it may be for only a while.
But if fight here we must,
Then in God is our trust.
So, send me away with a smile.

When I leave you dear,
Give me words of cheer,
To recall in times of pain.
They will come towards me,
And will seem to be,
Like the sunshine after rain.
Amid shot and shell,
I'd remember well.
You must be a soldier too.
And through this war I am fighting,
For my country, my home, and you.

REPEAT CHORUS.

'I'm Always Chasing Rainbows', 1917

Music: Harry Caroll. Lyrics: Jo McCarthy

Although the song was published in 1917 it was not introduced to the wider public until it appeared in the Broadway show *Oh, Look!* in March 1918. When it opened in London later that year it was a huge success. The melody is actually adapted from the *Fantaisie-Impromptu* by Frédéric Chopin.

At the end of the rainbow there's happiness,
And to find it how often I've tried,
But my life is a race, just a wild goose chase,
And my dreams have all been denied.
Why have I always been a failure?
What can the reason be?
I wonder if the world's to blame,
I wonder if it could be me.

I'm always chasing rainbows,
Watching clouds drifting by,
My dreams are just like all my schemes,
Ending in the sky.
Some fellows look and find the sunshine,
I always look and find the rain.
Some fellows make a winning sometime,
I never even make a gain, believe me,
I'm always chasing rainbows,
I'm watching for a little bluebird in vain.

'Till We Meet Again', 1918

Music: Richard A. Whiting. Lyrics: Raymond B. Egan

A song that became very popular towards the end of the war and showed that where the soldiers were concerned, sentimentality about home and loved ones had not diminished in the slightest.

There's a song in the land of the lily,
Each sweetheart has heard with a sigh.
Over high garden walls this sweet echo falls,
As a soldier boy whispers goodbye:

CHORUS:
Smile the while you kiss me sad adieu,
When the clouds roll by I'll come to you.
Then the skies will seem more blue,
Down in Lover's Lane, my dearie.

Wedding bells will ring so merrily
Ev'ry tear will be a memory.
So wait and pray each night for me
Till we meet again.

Tho' goodbye means the birth of a tear drop,
Hello means the birth of a smile.
And the smile will erase the tear blighting trace,
When we meet in the after awhile.

REPEAT CHORUS.

SONGS, CHANTS AND MONOLOGUES FROM THE TRENCHES

The songs sung in the line, or when relaxing in male company, were of a very different form to the popular songs imported from home and many were the direct product of trench warfare. 'Take Me Back To Dear Old Blighty' was written in 1916 by Bennett Scott who pointed out, 'That song comes straight from the trenches. Two years ago, it could not have existed.'*

In addition, there was a sizable element of the bawdy; arguably the most infamous being 'Mademoiselle From Armentières'. It is not known exactly how many verses there were; certainly over a dozen are known but

---

* R.A. Baker, *British Music Hall, An Illustrated History*, Sutton, Stroud, 2005, p.169.

inventive minds doubtless made up many more. These songs would rarely be sung in mixed company, except when the soldiers believed (often wrongly) that the French girls serving in the estaminets couldn't understand the words and they provided great amusement to men who were mostly starved of any female company. Coming from Britain, with its strict Victorian morality, men found themselves surrounded by French and Belgian women, many with no male partners, whom they found frighteningly open and sexually forward compared to English women and this is frequently reflected in the ribald and exaggerated nature of the songs.

Then there were many repetitive chants (one can hardly call them songs) that defy any form of musical classification. Although they were frequently sung on the march, more often they were repeated by one or more men when undertaking routine trench fatigues, such as filling sandbags or carrying rations or during more social times, when men were sitting around relaxing. How they originated is not known; the majority seem to be based on existing songs with words probably made up by a battalion wag. 'We're Here Because We're Here' is a lament with no real beginning or ending and 'Lloyd George Knew My Father', sung to the tune of 'Onward Christian Soldiers', is quite daft but was sung lustily and for fairly long periods of time while on the march, as its timing nicely matched the pace of the soldiers. They cover the entire gamut of emotions: crude, humorous, cynical and just plain nonsensical.

Finally there are the monologues, and although not numerous, they too were very popular. Most were imported from vaudeville acts and a few could be sung and they contained that indefinable element of self-deprecatory English humour that was so utterly incomprehensible to other nations. Probably their apogee was the patter used by the soldiers who ran the game of House. Soldiers who could repeat any of the monologues without fault were usually bought beers for the rest of the evening.

Most of these trench songs have many variants, their authors are anonymous and none are possible to date with any accuracy, so I have used the most commonly found versions and noted the original tune, where possible. As it is impossible to put them into any chronology the trench songs are in alphabetical order.

'A Shilling A Day'

This rather cynical chant certainly existed well before the Great War, and may possibly date back to the 18th century.

> Come and be a soldier, lads,
> Come, lads, come.
> Hark – don't you hear
> The fife and the drum?
> Come to the battlefield,
> March, march away,
> Come and lose your eyes and limbs,
> All for a shilling a day.
>
> Remember we are soldiers, lads,
> The bravest of the brave.
> Come and be a soldier,
> Then you'll also be a slave.
> Stand before the colonel, lads,
> But don't you dare to cry.
> Though none of you are happy, lads,
> They can flog you 'til you die.

'And When I Die'

A little nonsense song usually sung by two men, the second repeating the refrain *sotto voce*. It was sung to the author by ex-Private Clarrie Jarman, who accompanied it on his mouth organ. A curious song for him to recall, as he was a lifelong teetotaller!

And when I die,
Don't bury me.
Just pickle my toes,
In alcohol,
With a bottle of booze
At my head and my feet.
And then I'll know
My toes will keep.

'Après La Guerre Fini'

Tune: 'Under The Bridges Of Paris'

A fine example of what is now known as 'Franglais' it illustrated how the British soldiers, inevitably tongue-tied by any hint of a foreign language, dealt with French.

Après la guerre fini,
Soldat anglais parti.
Mam'selle Fransay boko pleuray,
Après la guerre fini.

Après la guerre fini,
Soldat anglais parti.
Mademoiselle in the family way,
Après la guerre fini.

Après la guerre fini,
Soldat anglais parti.
Mademoiselle can go to hell,
Après la guerre fini.

'Archibald! Certainly Not'

This music-hall monologue was made famous by George Robey, who recited it with great emphasis on the innuendo it contained. Robey raised half a million pounds for charity during the war and received a knighthood. The term 'Archie' was adopted by the Royal Flying Corps in 1915 as vernacular for German anti-aircraft fire and was allegedly so named after a pilot named 'Biffy' Borton who sang out the chorus whenever bursts of anti-aircraft exploded near his machine, much to the puzzlement of his NCO observer.

It's no use me denying facts, I'm henpecked, you can see!
'Twas on our wedding day my wife commenced to peck at me.
The wedding breakfast over, I said, 'We'll start off today
Upon our honeymoon.'
Then she yelled, 'What! waste time that way?'

'Archibald, certainly not!
Get back to work at once, sir, like a shot.
When single you could waste time spooning
But lose work now for honeymooning!
Archibald, certainly not!'

I once strolled through a field, and there a mad bull came across.
It gamboll'd with me playfully and quickly won the toss!
Of course I sued the owner, and the day the case was fought,
The judge exclaimed when I said, 'Sir, let's have the bull in court!'

'Archibald, certainly not!
Just show what other evidence you've got!'

But he cried when I said, 'Please forgo it…
Because I must stand up to show it.'
'Archibald, certainly not!'

A sportsman I have always been, I've hunted with the hounds.
I've hunted, too, without them, and it's cost me many pounds.
I can't afford to hunt now that I'm married, but one day,
The wife remarked, when I asked her if cricket I could play,

'Archibald, certainly not!
About this cricket game I've read a lot.
Besides, last time you played at Dover,
I heard you bowled a maiden over!
Archibald, certainly not!'

A lady named Miss Hewitt got on friendly terms with me.
She fell in love with me at once and then fell in the sea!
My wife came on the scene as I threw coat and vest aside;
As other garments I slipped off to save the girl, she cried,

'Archibald, certainly not!
Desist at once disrobing on the spot!
You may show your pluck and save Miss Hewitt,
But if you've got to strip to do it,
Archibald, certainly not!'

At supper time last Sunday I was hungry as could be.
A chicken on the table smelt most savoury to me!
I longed for just a taster as I munched my jam and bread.
At last I said, 'Can I have just the beak?' then my wife said,

'Archibald, certainly not!

You know that fowl for you was never got.
Eat chicken when to bed you're going!
Why, all night long I'd have you crowing!
Archibald, certainly not!'

'At The Halt'

Tune: 'Three Cheers For The Red, White And Blue'

At the halt on the left, form platoon,
At the halt on the left, form platoon,
If the off numbers don't mark time in two places,
How the hell can the rest form platoon?

"Faster? No, I ain't goin' no faster, young 'igh velocity. I ain't got but two
speeds, slow and stop." (Punch)

'Barney'

Tune: 'Bring Back My Bonnie To Me'

I took my girl for a ramble,
We went down a wee shady lane.
She caught her foot in a bramble,
And arse over tits she came.

Oh Barney,
Oh Barney,
Oh bring back my Barney to me, to me.
Oh Barney, oh Barney,
Oh bring back my Barney to me.

'Bombed Last Night'

A similar, shortened version entitled 'Glorious' also exists. This cheery tune was based on a traditional English jig.

Bombed last night, and bombed the night before,
Going to get bombed tonight, if we never get bombed any more.
When we're bombed, we're scared as we can be,
Can't stop the bombing sent from higher Germany.

They're over us, they're over us,
One shell hole for just the four of us.
Thank your lucky stars there are no more of us,
'Cause one of us can fill it all alone.

Gassed last night, and gassed the night before,
Going to get gassed tonight, if we never get gassed anymore.
When we're gassed, we're sick as we can be,
For Phosgene and Mustard Gas is much too much for me.

They're warning us, they're warning us,
One respirator for the four of us.
Thank your lucky stars that three of us can run,
So one of us can use it all alone.

Shelled last night, and shelled the night before,
Going to get shelled tonight, if we never get shelled anymore.
When we're shelled, we're windy as we can be,
'Cos we can't stop the shells coming from Germany.

They're warning us, they're warning us,
One tin hat between the four of us.
Soon there won't be any more of us
Only the tin hat all alone.

'Can We Clean Your Windows?'

The expletive in the last but one line was often
substituted by something less ribald, such as 'dash it', if
the chant was sung in mixed company.

Can we clean your windows, mum?
We'll make 'em shine,
Bloody fine.
Not today,
Go Away!

'All right' says poor Jim,
As he threw down his bucket,
And he called out 'Oh fuck it',
Can we clean your windows Mum?

'Casey Jones'

Tune: 'Casey Jones'

A traditional American song, modified for trench warfare.

Casey Jones,
Standing on the fire-step,
Casey Jones
A pistol in his hand,
Casey Jones,
Standing on the fire step,
Firing Very lights into No-Man's Land.

'Charlie Chaplin'

Tune: 'Little Redwing'

Chaplin was internationally popular and his silent films resulted in record audiences at cinemas. His 1918 film *Shoulder Arms* was the first ever to treat the subject of war in a humorous fashion.

Oh, the moon shines down
On Charlie Chaplin,

He's going barmy
To join the army.
But his little baggy trousers
They need a-mending,
Before they send him
To the Dardanelles.

Oh, the moon shines bright
On Charlie Chaplin,
But his shoes are cracking
For want of blacking,
And his baggy khaki trousers
Still need a-mending,
Before they send him
To the Dardanelles.

'Dan, Dan, The Sanitary Man'

Dan, Dan, the sanitary man,
Working underground all day.
Sweeping up urinals,
Picking out the finals,
Whiling happy hours away, gor blimey!
Doing his little bit,
Shovelling up the shit,
He is so blithe and gay.
And the only music that he hears
Is poo-poo-poo-poo all day.

'Do Your Balls Hang High?'

Tune: 'The Sailors' Hornpipe'

Do your balls hang high,
Do your balls hang low,
Can you tie them in a knot?
Can you tie them in a bow?
Do you get a funny feeling
If you slap 'em on the ceiling?
Oh, you'll never make a sailor if your balls hang low!

'Don't Send Me (The Conshie's Song)'

Written by D. Burnaby and G. Rice, 1917

This began life as a humorous music-hall monologue and as the war continued it developed a momentum of its own. The camp lyrics were so far removed from reality that they merely added to its amusement. The final verse would often be heard sung out with particular enthusiasm during a march or when performing fatigues.

Perhaps you wonder what I am,
I will explain to you,
My conscience is the only thing,
That helps to pull me through.
Objection is a thing that I
Have studied thoroughly.
I don't object to fighting Huns,
But should hate them fighting me.

CHORUS:

Send out the Army and the Navy,
Send out the rank and file,
Send out the brave old Territorials,
They'll face the danger with a smile.
Send out the boys of the Old Brigade,
Who made Old England free.
Send out me brother, his sister and his mother,
But for Gawd's sake don't send me.

Non-combatant battalions
Are fairly in my line,
But the sergeant always hates me,
And he calls me 'Baby mine'.
But oh, I got so cross with him,
I rose to the attack,
And when he called me 'Ethel'
I just called him 'Beatrice' back!

REPEAT CHORUS.

We have a nasty officer,
He is a horrid brute
Last Friday he was terse with me,
'Cos I did not salute.
But I cut him twice today,
Then he asked the reason please?
I said, 'I thought, dear Captain,
That you still were cross with me.'

REPEAT CHORUS.

306

'Far, Far From Wipers'

Tune: 'Sing Me To Sleep, Mother Dear'

One of the few songs that was location-specific, Ypres having a particular place in the minds of any soldiers who served in the infamous Salient. Generally, that place was a nightmare.

Far, far from Wipers,
I long to be.
Where German snipers
Can't shoot at me.
Wet is my dug-out,
Damp are my feet,
Waiting for whizz-bangs
To send me to sleep.

'Father's Pants'

Tune: 'Bread Of Heaven'

Another of the many repetitious songs sung until the soldiers tired of it.

Father's pants will soon fit Willie.
Will he wear them?
Will he hell!
Will he wear them? Will he wear them? Will he wear them?
Will he hell!
Will he wear them?

THE NEUVE EGLISE HIPPODROME

GRAND NEW REVIEW, ENTITLED:

"SHELL IN"

POSITIVELY THE GREATEST SPECTACULAR PERFORMANCE EVER STAGED.

BRINGING BEFORE THE PUBLIC AT ONE AND THE SAME TIME THE
FOLLOWING HIGHLY-PAID STARS:

THE CRUMPS.

LITTLE PIP-SQUEAK

DUDDY WHIZZ-BANG.

HURLA SHELLOG, etc., etc.

THRILLING OPENING CHORUS ARRANGED BY LEWIS VICKERS.

Exciting! Hair-raising!! Awe-inspiring!!!

SEE WHAT THE PAPERS SAY.   BOOK EARLY.   PRICES DOUBLE THIS WEEK.

TO HARASSED SUBALTERNS.

—o—o—o—o—

IS YOUR LIFE MISERABLE? ARE YOU UNHAPPY?

DO YOU HATE YOUR COMPANY COMMANDER?

—o—o—o—o—

YES! THEN BUY HIM ONE OF

OUR NEW PATENT TIP DUCK BOARDS

YOU GET HIM ON THE END—THE DUCK BOARD DOES THE REST

—o—o—o—o—

Made in three sizes, and every time a "Blighty."

—o—o—o—o—

" It once he steps on to the end,
'Twill take a month his face to mend "

—o—o— o—o—

WRITE AT ONCE & ENSURE HAPPINESS

THE NOVELTY SYNDICATE, R.E. HOUSE   Tel.: " Dump'

(Author's collection)

Will he hell!
Father's pants will soon ... *(repeated endlessly or until exhausted)*

'Fred Karno's Army'

Tune: 'The Church's One Foundation'

As with many other songs incorporating swear words, 'fuck' in the fourth line was sometimes substituted by 'shoot'.

We are Fred Karno's Army,
The ragtime infantry.
We cannot fight,
We cannot fuck,
What bleedin' use are we?

And when we get to Berlin,
The Kaiser he will say,
'Hoch, hoch, mein Gott,
What a bloody rotten lot,
Are the ragtime infantry.'

'Fred Karno's Army' – the RFC / RAF version

We are Fred Karno's airforce,
Fred Karno's our OC.
Charlie Chaplin is our captain,
What a funny lot are we.

And when we get to Berlin,

> The Kaiser, he will say,
> 'Hoch, hoch, mein Gott
> What a bloody funny lot
> Are the men of the RFC.'

'Forward Joe Soap's Army'

Tune: 'Onward Christian Soldiers'

Sometimes sung in parallel with the proper hymn during church parades, despite dire consequences being threatened for any man overhead doing so by his NCOs or officers!

> Forward Joe Soap's army, marching without fear,
> With our old commander, safely in the rear.
> He boasts and skites from morn till night,
> And thinks he's very brave,
> But the men who really did the job are dead and in their grave.
> Forward Joe Soap's army, marching without fear,
> With our old commander, safely in the rear.
> Amen.

'Gallipoli's A Wonderful Place'

Tune: 'The Mountains Of Mourne'

Oh, old Gallipoli's a wonderful place,
Where the boys in the trenches the foe have to face,
But they never grumble, they smile through it all,
Very soon they expect Achi Baba to fall.
At least when I asked them, that's what they told me,
In Constantinople quite soon we would be,
But if war lasts till Doomsday I think we'll still be,
Where the old Gallipoli sweeps down to the sea.

We don't grow potatoes or barley or wheat,
So we're on the lookout for something to eat,
We're fed up with biscuits and bully and ham,
And we're sick of the sight of yon parapet jam.
Send out steak and onions and nice ham and eggs,
And a fine big fat chicken with five or six legs,
And a drink of the stuff that begins with a 'B',
Where the old Gallipoli sweeps down to the sea.

'General Shute'

Tune: 'Wrap Me In My Tarpaulin Jacket'

One of the rare works that can be specifically ascribed to someone, in this case two people. It was penned by Lieutenant A.P. Herbert of the Royal Naval Division in 1916 (who later became a prominent author) about its Commanding Officer, Major Sir Cameron Shute, who had a particular dislike for the naval traditions of the RND. It became hugely popular throughout the division.

The General inspecting the trenches,
Exclaimed with a horrified shout,
'I refuse to inspect a division
Which leaves its excreta about.'
But nobody took any notice,
No one was prepared to refute,
That the presence of shit was congenial,
Compared with the presence of Shute.

And certain responsible critics
Made haste to reply to his words,
Observing his staff of advisers
Consisted entirely of turds.
For shit may be shot at odd corners,
And paper supplied there to suit,
But shit would be shot without mourners,
If somebody shot that shit Shute.

'Glorious'

There were doubtless many verses of this, but only the following have survived.

> Glorious! Glorious!
> One bottle of beer between the four of us,
> Thank Gawd that there are no more of us,
> So none of us can drink it on his own.

> Glorious! Glorious!
> One tin hat between the four of us,
> Thank Gawd that there are no more of us,
> And one of us can wear it at a time.

> Glorious! Glorious!
> One gas mask between the four of us,
> Thank Gawd that there are no more of us,
> Or three of us would have to run away.

'Good-Bye Nellie'

Tune: Traditional

This song originated around the time of the Boer War and despite its rather old fashioned sentiments it remained a particularly popular tune when sung at divisional concert parties.

Good-bye Nellie,
I'm going across the main.
Farewell Nellie,
This parting gives me pain.
I shall always love you,
As true as the stars above.
I'm going to do my duty,
For the girl I love.

'Here's To The Good Old Beer'

A very popular pre-war drinking song, possibly originating from Lincolnshire. There are as many verses as there are different drinks.

Here's to the good old beer,
Mop it down, mop it down.
Here's to the good old beer,
Mop it down.
Here's to the good old beer,
That never leaves you queer,
Here's to the good old beer,
Mop it down.

Here's to the good old whiskey,
Mop it down, mop it down.
Here's to the good old whiskey,
Mop it down.
Here's to the good old whiskey,
That makes you feel so frisky,
Here's to the good old whiskey,
Mop it down.

Here's to the good old stout,
Mop it down, mop it down.
Here's to the good old stout,
Mop it down.
Here's to the good old stout,
That makes you feel blown-out,
Here's to the good old stout,
Mop it down.

Here's to the good old brandy,
Mop it down, mop it down.
Here's to the good old brandy,
Mop it down.
Here's to the good old brandy,
That leaves you feeling randy,
Here's to the good old brandy,
Mop it down.

Here's to the good old rum,
Mop it down, mop it down.
Here's to the good old rum,
Mop it down.
Here's to the good old rum,
That that warms your balls and bum,
Here's to the good old rum,
Mop it down.

Here's to the good old porter,
Mop it down, mop it down.
Here's to the good old porter,
Mop it down.
Here's to the good old porter,
That slips down like it 'oughter,
Here's to the good old porter,
Mop it down.

'Here's To The Next Man Who Dies'

An RFC/RAF song, taken from a 19th-century Irish poem called 'The Revel'. Losses among aircrew were extremely high, and pilots developed a black humour about their possibilities of survival. In 1917, the average new pilot's life expectancy was two weeks.

We meet 'neath the sounding rafters,
And the walls around are bare.
As they echo to our laughter,
T'would seem that the dead were there.

So stand to your glasses steady,
'Tis all we have left to prize.
Quaff a cup to the dead already,
And one to the next man who dies.

Time was when we frowned on others,
We thought we were wiser then.
But now let us all be brothers,
For we never may meet again.

Cut off from the land that bore us,
Betrayed by the land we find,
The good men have gone before us,
And only the dull left behind.

So stand to your glasses steady,
This world is a web of lies.
Then here's to the dead already,
And hurrah for the next man who dies.

We meet 'neath the sounding rafter,
And the walls around are bare.
As they shout back our peals of laughter,
It seems that the dead are there.

Then stand to your glasses steady,
We drink in our comrades' eyes.
One cup to the dead already,
Hurrah for the next man that dies.

We loop in the purple twilight,
We spin in the silvery dawn,
With a trail of smoke behind us,
To show where our comrades have gone.

So, stand to your glasses steady,
This world is a world full of lies.
Here's a toast to those dead already,
And here's to the next man to die.

Here's an end to this mournful story
For death is a distant friend,
So here's to a life of glory,
And a laurel to crown each end.
Here's a toast to those dead already,
And here's to the next man to die.

'He's A Ragtime Soldier'

Tune: 'Ragtime Lover'

During the war, ragtime music became all the rage, and many songs and tunes reflected the new craze.

He's a ragtime soldier,
Ragtime soldier,
Early on parade every morning,
Standing to attention with his rifle in his hand.
He's a ragtime soldier,
As happy as the flowers in May
(I don't think!)
Fighting for his King and country,
All for a shilling a day.

'Hush – Here Comes A Whizz-Bang'

Tune: 'Here Comes The Dream Man'

A lighthearted song often sung in cafes and estaminets, where the tables could be given a resounding thump when the last line was reached.

Hush! Here comes a whizz-bang,
Hush! Here comes a whizz-bang,
Down you soldiers, get down those stairs,
Down in your dug-outs,
And say your prayers.
Hush! Here comes a whizz-bang,
And it's making straight for you,
And you'll see all the wonders
Of No-Man's Land,
If a whizz-bang (**thump**) hits you.

'I Don't Want To Join The Army (I Don't Want To Be A Soldier)'

I don't want to join the army,
I don't want to go to war,
I'd rather stay at home,
Around the streets to roam,
Living on the earnings of a nice young lady.
I don't want a bayonet up my arsehole,
I don't want my bollocks shot away,
I'd rather stay in England,

Merry, merry England,
And fornicate my bleedin' life away.

I don't want to be a soldier,
I don't want to go to war.
I'd rather hang around
Piccadilly underground,
And live off the earnings
Of a high born lady.
I don't need no Froggy women,
London's full of girls I've never had.
Dear oh Gawd almighty,
I want to stay in Blighty
And follow in the footsteps of me dad.

'I Have No Pain, Mother Dear'

Yet another little chant on the very popular subject of alcohol.

I have no pain, mother dear, now,
But oh, I am so dry.
Connect me to a brewery,
And leave me there to die.

'I'm A General At The Ministry'

Tune: Gilbert and Sullivan, 'I Am The Ruler Of The Queen's Navy'

A complex RFC song that, like its army counterparts, poked fun at the hierarchy and the apparent inability of staff officers to do anything even remotely useful.

When I was a lad I went to war,
As an air mechanic in the Flying Corps.
I dished out dope, and I swung the prop,
And I polished up my talents in the fitter's shop;
And I did my work so carefully,
That now I'm a general at the Ministry.

As an air mechanic I made such a name,
A sergeant major I soon became.
I wore a tunic and Sam Browne belt,
And my presence on parade was most acutely felt.
My presence was felt so overwhelmingly,
That now I'm the general at the Ministry.

As a sergeant major I made such a hit,
That I demanded further scope to do my bit;
Of my lofty ways there was never any doubt,
And they sent me up in a Nieuport Scout.
I flew so well over land and sea,
That now I'm the general at the Ministry.

I flew in France with such amazing zest,
That the King grew tired of adorning my chest.

322

People boosted McCudden, Bishop and Ball,
But readily agreed that I out-soared them all.
My merits were declared so overwhelmingly,
That now I'm a general at the Ministry.

So mechanics all, wherever you be,
If you want to climb to the top of the tree,
If your soul isn't fettered to a pail of dope,
Just take my tip – there's always hope.
Be smart in the Strand at saluting me,
And you'll be a general at the Ministry.

'I Want To Go Home'

A very popular trench song, often sung on the march,
as it is quite a merry tune. The soldiers meant every
word.

I want to go home. I want to go home.
I don't want to go in the trenches no more,
Where whizz-bangs and shrapnel
They whistle and roar.
Take me over the sea,
Where the Alleyman can't get at me.
Oh my! I don't want to die.
I want to go home.
I want to go home, I want to go home.
Bullets and shrapnel they whistle and roar,
I don't want to go in the trenches no more.
I want to go over the sea,
Where the Kaiser can't shoot bombs at me.

Oh my! I don't want to die.

I want to go home.

'I Wish I Was Single'

I wish I was single again.

I wish I was single again.

For when I was single,

My pockets would jingle.

Oh, I wish I was single again.

'I Wore A Tunic'

Tune: 'I Wore A Tulip'

This was a harsh song about the shirkers and profiteers who remained in Britain during the war.

I wore a tunic; a dirty khaki tunic,

And you wore your civvie clothes.

We fought and bled at Loos,

While you were on the booze,

The booze that no-one here knows.

You were with the wenches,

While we were in the trenches,

Facing an angry foe.

Oh you were a-slacking,

While we were attacking

The Germans on the Menin road.

THE

WIPERS TIMES.

OR

SALIENT NEWS.

| No 4. Vol. 2. | Monday. 20th March, 1916. | Price 50 Centimes. |

HAS YOUR BOY A MECHANICAL TURN OF MIND? YES!

—o—o—o—o—

THEN BUY HIM A

FLAMMENWERFER

INSTRUCTIVE—AMUSING.

—o—o—o—o—

Both young and old enjoy,
This nasty little toy.

—o—o—o—o—

GUARANTEED ABSOLUTELY HARMLESS

—o—o—o—o—

Thousands Have Been Sold.

—o—o—o—o—

Drop a postcard to Messrs. ARMY, RESEARCH and CO., when a handsome illustrated
catalogue will be sent you.

(Author's collection)

325

'If The Sergeant Steals Your Rum (Never Mind)'

Typical of the nature of the front-line soldier, whose attitude after a few months of trench life usually became a fatalistic 'If it happens, it happens'.

If the sergeant steals your rum, never mind.
If the sergeant steals your rum, never mind.
Though he's just a bloody sot,
Let him take the bleedin' lot,
If the sergeant steals your rum,
Never mind.

If old Jerry shells the trench, never mind.
If old Jerry shells the trench, never mind.
Though the blasted sandbags fly,
You have only once to die,
If old jerry shells the trench,
Never mind.

If you get stuck on the wire, never mind.
If you get stuck on the wire, never mind.
Though the light's as broad as day,
When you die,
They'll stop your pay.
If you get stuck on the wire,
Never mind.

'It Was Christmas Day In The Workhouse'

There were several versions of this, all along similar lines and the three best known are reproduced here. Depending on the audience, instead of the bawdy last four lines of each verse, the refrain 'Tidings of comfort and joy, comfort and joy, all glad tidings of comfort and joy' was sometimes substituted.

(Version 1)

It was Christmas Day in the workhouse,
The season of good cheer.
The paupers' hearts were merry,
Their bellies full of beer.
The pompous workhouse master
As he strode about the halls,
Wished them a Merry Christmas,
But the paupers answered 'balls'.
This angered the workhouse master
Who swore by all the gods,
That he'd stop their Christmas pudden,
The rotten little sods.

Then up spake a wizened pauper,
His face as bold as brass,
'You can keep your Christmas pudden' mate,
And stick it up your arse.'

(Version 2)

It was Christmas Day in the cookhouse,
The happiest day of the year.
Men's hearts were full of gladness,

And their bellies full of beer.
The pompous sergeant major
Strode round the dining halls,
He wished them a merry Christmas
But the soldiers shouted 'balls'.
This angered the sergeant major
Who swore by the army gods,
That he'd stop their Christmas pudden'
The ungrateful little sods.

When up spoke Private Shortarse,
His face as bold as brass,
Saying, 'You can take your fuckin' pudden, Sarge,
and shove it up your arse.'

(Version 3)
It was Christmas day in the harem,
The eunuchs was standing around,
And hundreds of beautiful women
Were stretched out on the ground,
When in walked the bold bad sultan,
And strode through his marble halls,
Asking 'What do you want for Christmas, boys?'
And the eunuchs answered:
'Balls!'

'I've Lost My Rifle'

Tune: 'Since I Lost You'

I've lost my rifle and bayonet,
I've lost my pull-through too.
I've lost my disc and my puttees,
I've lost my four by two.
I've lost my housewife and hold-all,
I've lost my button stick too,
I've lost my rations and greatcoat,
Sergeant what shall I do?

'John Brown's Baby'

Tune: 'John Brown's Body'

The word 'arse' was sometimes substituted by 'hush!'

John Brown's baby has a pimple on his arse.
John Brown's baby has a pimple on his arse.
John Brown's baby has a pimple on his arse.
And the poor child can't sit down.

'Kaiser Bill'

Tune: 'Pop Goes The Weasel'

Kaiser Bill is feeling ill,
The Crown Prince, he's gone barmy.
We don't give a fuck for old von Kluck,
And all his bleeding army.

'Mademoiselle From Armentières (Inkey Dinkey Parlez-Vous)'

Possibly the most infamous and certainly one of the longest First World War songs; no-one really knows today how many verses or variants there were. One veteran assured the author he knew 26 verses, but was no longer able to recall them! Some were so obscene that even today they would raise eyebrows if published. Two very different versions are reproduced here.

(The sanitized version)
Three German officers crossed the line, parlez-vous.
Three German officers crossed the line, parlez-vous.
Three German officers crossed the line,
On the lookout for women and wine.
Inkey dinky parlez-vous.

They came to an inn on top of a rise, parlez-vous.
A famous inn of bloody great size, parlez-vous.
They saw a maid all dimples and sighs,
They both agreed she'd lovely eyes.

Inkey dinky parlez-vous.

Oh landlord, you've a daughter fair, parlez-vous.
Oh landlord, you've a daughter fair, parlez-vous.
Oh landlord, you've a daughter fair,
With lily white tits and golden hair.
Inkey dinky parlez-vous.

Nein, nein, mein Herr, she's much too young, parlez-vous.
Nein, nein, mein Herr, she's much too young, parlez-vous.
Mais non, mon père, I'm not too young,
I've often slept with the parson's son.
Inkey dinky parlez-vous.

The rest of the tale I can't relate, parlez-vous.
It's a very old story but bang up to date, parlez-vous.
The story of man seducing a maid,
It could offend – you're too sedate.
Inkey dinky parlez-vous.

(One of the bawdy versions)
Three German soldiers crossed the Rhine, parlez-vous.
Three German soldiers crossed the Rhine, parlez-vous.
Three German soldiers crossed the Rhine,

To fuck the women and drink the wine.
Inky dinky parlez-vous.

They came to the door of a wayside inn, parlez-vous.
Pissed on the mat and walked right in, parlez-vous.
Inky dinky parlez-vous.
'Oh landlord, have you a daughter fair?', parlez-vous.

'With lily-white tits and golden hair?', parlez-vous.
Inky dinky parlez-vous.

'My only daughter's far too young', parlez-vous.
'To be fucked by you, you bastard hun,' parlez-vous.
Inky dinky parlez-vous.

'Oh father dear I'm not too young,' parlez-vous.
'I've just been fucked by the blacksmith's son', parlez-vous.
Inky dinky parlez-vous.

At last they got her on the bed, parlez-vous.
And shagged her 'til her cheeks were red, parlez-vous.
Inky dinky parlez-vous.

And then they found a bigger bed, parlez-vous.
And shagged her 'til she was nearly dead, parlez-vous.
Inky dinky parlez-vous.

They took her down a shady lane, parlez-vous.
And shagged her back to life again, parlez-vous.
Inky dinky parlez-vous.

They shagged her up, they shagged her down, parlez-vous.
They shagged her all around the town, parlez-vous.
Inky dinky parlez-vous.

They shagged her in, they shagged her out, parlez-vous.
They shagged her up her water-spout, parlez-vous.
Inky dinky parlez-vous.

Now seven months later all was well, parlez-vous.
Eight months later she began to swell, parlez-vous.
Inky dinky parlez-vous.

Nine months later she gave a heave, parlez-vous.
And a little fat Prussian popped out between her knees, parlez-vous.
Inky dinky parlez-vous.

The fat little Prussian he grew and grew, parlez-vous.
He fucked the cat and the donkey too, parlez-vous.
Inky dinky parlez-vous.

The fat little Prussian he went to hell, parlez-vous.
Where he fucked the devil's wife as well, parlez-vous.
Inky dinky parlez-vous.

'Michael Finnigan'

A children's street chant

Poor old Michael Finnegan,
He grew whiskers on his chinnigan.
Shaved them off and they grew in ag'in,
And that's the end of poor Michael Finnegan.

'Miles Behind The Lines'

Tune: Probably 'I Wore A Red, Red Rose'

We had a windy sergeant,

A very windy sergeant.

Early every morning,

When we were standing to,

He was pottering in the dug-out,

With his four by two,

Miles behind the lines.

And we had a sergeant major,

Who never fired a gun,

And he got the DCM,

For things he never done.

And mentioned in dispatches,

For drinking privates' rum,

And when he sees the Alleyman,

You should see the bastard run,

Miles and miles behind the lines.

'My Nelly'

Tune: 'Three Blind Mice'

My Nelly's a whore,
My Nelly's a whore,
She's got such wonderful eyes of blue,
She uses such wonderful language too,
Her favourite expression is 'bollocks to you',
My Nelly's a whore.

'My Old Man's A Guardsman'

A modified version of a 19th-century street rhyme. This was repeated to the author by a Mons veteran and there were more verses than he was able to recall. If it seems familiar, the tune gained fame in the 1960s when it appeared, as 'My Old Man's A Dustman' in a skiffle version sung by Lonnie Donnegan.

My old man's a guardsman,
He fought at the battle of Mons.
He killed a dozen Germans,
With only a couple of bombs.
The Bosche fought hard,
The Bosche fought well,
The Bosche soon pushed us back.
But my old man decided
The Bosche he would attack.
He was a one-man army,
And he killed the bleedin' lot.

One lay here, and one lay there,

And one around the corner.

And another poor sod with his leg hanging off

Was crying out for water.

But my old man's a guardsman,

'E's tough as leather boots,

And when he sees a German

His rifle quick he shoots.

And when he leaves the trench that night,

The Bosches they was dead,

And he's one of their spiky helmets,

A-sitting on his head.

'Never Trust a Sailor'

Tune: 'Oh Susannah'

Once I was a skivvy,

Down in Drury Lane,

And I used to love the mistress

And the master just the same.

One day came a sailor,

A sailor from the sea,

And he was the cause

Of all my misery.

He asked me for a candle,

To light him up to bed.

He asked me for a pillow,

To rest his weary head.

Directing the Way at the Front.
"Yer knows the dead 'orse 'cross the road? Well, keep straight on till yer comes to a p'rambulator 'longside a Johnson 'ole." (Bruce Bairnsfather, author's collection)

And I being young and
Innocent of harm,
Jumped into bed,
Just to keep the sailor warm.

And next morning,
When I awoke,
He handed me
A five pound note.

Take this my dear,
For the damage I have done.
It may be a daughter,
Or it may be a son.

If it be a daughter,
Bounce her on your knee.
If it be a son,
Send the bastard off to sea.

Bell-bottomed trousers,
And a coat of blue,
And make him climb the rigging
As his daddy climbed up you.

So never trust a sailor
An inch above your knee.
I did and he left me
With a bastard on my knee.

'Nobody Knows'

Usually sung with great emotion at the end of a long march.

Nobody knows how tired we are,
Tired we are,
Tired we are.
Nobody knows how tired we are,
And nobody seems to care.

Nobody knows how thirsty we are,
Thirsty we are,
Thirsty we are.
Nobody knows how thirsty we are,
And nobody seems to care.

Nobody knows how hungry we are,
Hungry we are,
Hungry we are.
Nobody knows how hungry we are,
And nobody seems to care.

'Old Mother Riley'

Old Mother Riley had a little kid,
Poor little blighter.
He wasn't very big,
And he wasn't very small,
Poor little blighter,
He only had one ball.

'Old Soldiers Never Die'

Tune: 'Kind Thoughts Can Never Die'

Old soldiers never die,
Never die, never die,
Old soldiers never die,
They simply fade away.

Old soldiers never die,
Never die, never die,
Old soldiers never die,
The young ones wish they would!

(Another verse is)
This rain will never stop,
Never stop,
Never stop,
This rain will never stop
No, oh, no, no, no.

'Our Little Wet Trench'

Tune: 'In My Little Grey Home In The West'

In our little wet home in the trench,
That the rain storms continually drench,
There's a dead cow near-by with its hooves in the sky,
And it gives off a terrible stench.
Beneath us instead of a floor,
Is a layer of cold mud and some straw.
The Jack Johnsons we dread,
As they speed overhead,
In our little wet home in the trench.

'Plum And Apple'

Tune: 'A Wee Deoch And Doris'

A song about the soldiers' obsession with Tickler's plum
and apple jam.

Plum and apple,
Apple and plum,
Plum and apple,
There's always some.

The ASC get strawberry jam,
And lashings of rum,
But we poor blokes
We only get –
apple and plum.

'Raining, Raining, Raining…'

Tune: 'Holy, Holy, Holy'

There was no limit to things soldiers could find to grouse about, and this song reflected just a few of them. It could be repeated, with different variations almost without end.

Raining, raining, raining,
Always bloody well raining.
Raining all the morning,
And raining all the night.

Grousing, grousing, grousing,
Always bloody well grousing.
Grousing at the rations,
And grousing at the pay.

Marching, marching, marching,
Always bloody well marching.
Marching all the night-time,
And marching all the day.

Fighting, fighting, fighting,
Always bloody well fighting.
Fighting all the morning,
And fighting all the night.

'Rolling Home'

This was frequently sung when coming out of the line and men's spirits were lifting.

Rolling home,

Rolling home,

Rolling home,

Rolling home,

By the light of the silvery moooo-oon,

Happy is the day,

When you draw some buckshee pay,

And you're rolling, rolling, rolling home.

'Rooty'

Tune: 'My Old Man's A Guardsman'

At times we gets some rooty,

To civvies known as bread.

It ain't as light as 'fevers' [feathers],

And it ain't exactly lead.

But we gets it down us somehow,

And we never sends it back,

Though it's covered up with whiskers,

What's rubbed off from the sack.

We gets no eggs for breakfast,

They sends us over shells,

And we dives into our dug-outs,

And we don't care if they smells.

'She Married A Man'

The squire had a daughter, so fair, so tall,
She lived in her satins and silks at the hall,
But she married a man,
With no balls at all.
No balls at all,
No balls at all,
She married a man who had no balls at all.

'She Was Poor But She Was Honest'

A traditional music-hall monologue from the 1880s.
Sometimes known as 'It's All The Same'.

She was poor, but she was honest,
Though she came from 'umble stock,
And an honest heart was beating,
Underneath her tattered frock.

'Eedless of 'er mother's warning,
Up to London she 'ad gone,
Yearning for the bright lights gleaming,
'Eedless of temp-ta-shy-on.

But the rich man saw her beauty,
She knew not his base design.
And he took her to a hotel,
And bought her a small port wine.

Then the rich man took 'er ridin',
Wrecker of poor women's souls,
But the Devil was the chauffeur,
As she rode in his Royce Rolls.

In the rich man's arms she fluttered,
Like a bird with a broken wing,
But he loved 'er and he left 'er,
Now she hasn't got no ring.

It's the same the whole world over,
It's the poor what gets the blame,
It's the rich what gets the pleasure,
Ain't it all a bloomin' shame?

Time has flown, outcast and helpless,
In the street she stands and says,
While the snowflakes fall around 'er,
'Won't you buy my bootlaces?'

See him riding in a carriage,
Past the gutter where she stands,
He has made a stylish marriage,
While she wrings her ringless hands.

See him there at the theatre,
In the front row with the best,
While the girl that he has ruined,
Entertains a sordid guest.

See 'er on the bridge at midnight,
She says 'Farewell, blighted love',
There's a scream, a splash… Good 'eavens!
What is she a-doing of?

So they dragged 'er from the river,
Water from 'er clothes they wrung,
They all thought that she was drownded,
But the corpse got up and sung:

It's the same the whole world over,
It's the poor what gets the blame,
It's the rich what gets the pleasure,
Ain't it all a bloomin' shame?

'She Was So Good'

A nonsensical repetitive song that would be sung for as long as the men could manage. It was originally part of a much longer folk song.

She was so good and kind to me,
Just like one of the family,
I shall never forget,
The first time we met,
She was –
She was –
She –
Was so good and kind to me … etc

'Stand By Your Beds'

An RFC variant of the bugle call 'General Salute'.

Stand by your beds,
Here comes the Air Vice Marshall,
He's got several rings,
But he's only got one arsehole.

'The ASC Have Gone To War'

Another song reflecting the soldiers' rather unfair dislike of the Army Service Corps, although dislike is perhaps the wrong word – envy would be more accurate. The theme of jam yet again enters into this tune.

The ASC to the war have gone,
At the base at Havre you will find them.
Their shining spurs they have girded on;
But they have left their bayonets behind them.
'What's the sense,' cried the ASC,
'Of taking to France the damn things?
Their only use, it seems to me;
Is to open the Tommy's jam tins.'

But thank the Lord for ASC,
The pride and joy of the nation,
Who bring our bully and jam and tea,
And our Maconochie ration.
Here's good luck to the ASC,
Though if they'd never come, boys,

347

I bet we'd get all the strawberry,
Instead of apple and plum, boys

'The Bells Of Hell'

Tune: 'She Only Answered "Ting A ling"'

A jolly tune with a hard edge to it, poking fun at the bible-thumpers and underlining a soldier's hope that death would always happen to someone else.

The bells of hells go ting-a-ling-a-ling,
For you but not for me.
And the little devils how they sing-a-ling-a-ling,
For you but not for me.
Oh Death, where is thy sting-a-ling-a-ling,
Oh Grave thy victory.
The bells of hells go ting-a-ling-a-ling,
For you but not for me.

'The Emma-Gees Song'

Tune: 'Oh I Do Like To Be Beside The Seaside'

Sung to the author by Lieutenant Colonel Julius Caesar, late of the Machine Gun Corps.

Oh, I do like to be beside our Maxims,
Oh, I do like to be an Emma Gee,
Oh, I do like to stroll along the parapet,
Where the Vickers go 'rattity-tat-tat-tat'.
So just let me play with my machine guns,
And I'll be besides myself with glee,
We've a lot more guns inside that I would like to be beside,
Beside the front lines, an Emma Gee.

'The Last Long Mile'

They put us in the army,
And they handed us a pack.
They took away our nice new clothes,
And dressed us up in 'kak'.
They march'd us twenty miles or more,
To fit us for the war.
We didn't mind the nineteen,
But the last one made us sore.

CHORUS:
Oh, it's not the pack
That you carry on your back,
Nor the gun up on your shoulder,

"GADGETS."

(Punch)

Nor the five-inch crust of France's dirty dust,
That makes you feel your limbs are getting older.
It's not the load on the hard straight road,
That drives away your smile.
If the socks from your sister raise a thumping blister,
Then blame it on the last long mile.

One day we had manoeuvres on dear old Salisbury Plain,
We march'd and march'd and march'd and march'd,
Then march'd and march'd again.
And when we stopped we had holes in our socks,
And our boot-soles were a smokin'.
It's not the 'tramp, tramp, tramp',
Or the thought of home or camp,
That drives away your smile.
It's being beaten by that last long mile.

REPEAT CHORUS.

'The Machine Gunners' Lament'

Tune: 'The Bonny, Bonny Banks Of Loch Lomond'

I'll take the tripod,
And you take the gun,
And you'll be in action before me.
And if you get shot,
I'll take the bleedin' lot
And I'll eat your rations,
In the morning.

'The Old Barbed Wire'

Tune: 'The British Grenadier'

A cynical song that was not popular with senior officers and one of the few that the army tried, without much success, to stop men singing.

If you want to find the sergeant,
I know where he is, I know where he is, I know where he is.
If you want to find the sergeant, I know where he is,
He's lying on the canteen floor.
I've seen him, I've seen him, lying on the canteen floor,
I've seen him, I've seen him, lying on the canteen floor.

If you want to find the quarter-bloke,
I know where he is, I know where he is, I know where he is.
If you want to find the quarter-bloke, I know where he is,
He's miles and miles behind the line.
I've seen him, I've seen him, miles and miles and miles behind the line.
I've seen him, I've seen him, miles and miles and miles behind the line.

If you want the sergeant major,
I know where he is, I know where he is, I know where he is.
If you want the sergeant major, I know where he is.
He's tossing off the privates' rum.
I've seen him, I've seen him, tossing off the privates' rum.
I've seen him, I've seen him, tossing off the privates' rum.

If you want to find the CO,
I know where he is, I know where he is, I know where he is.
If you want to find the CO, I know where he is.

He is down in a deep dug-out.
I've seen him, I've seen him, down in a deep dug-out,
I've seen him, I've seen him, down in a deep dug-out.

If you want to find the old battalion,
I know where they are, I know where they are, I know where they
are.
If you want to find the old battalion, I know where they are.
They're hanging on the old barbed wire.
I've seen 'em, I've seen 'em, hanging on the old barbed wire.
I've seen 'em, I've seen 'em, hanging on the old barbed wire.

'The Old French Trench'

Oh what a life, living in a trench,
Under Johnny French in an old French trench.
We haven't got a wife or a nice little wench,
But we're all still alive in this old French trench.

'The Sergeant's Greeting'

Seldom actually sung in the presence of the sergeant,
more often *sotto voce* – under the breath.

You've got a king face, you old bastard,
You ought to be bloody well shot.
You ought to be tied to a gun wheel,
And left there to bloody well rot.

'The Sergeant's Song'

Tune: 'Bring Back My Bonnie To Me'

Last night as I lay on my pillow,
Last night as I lay on my bed,
I dreamt our old sergeant was dying,
I dreamt that the old sod was dead.

CHORUS:
Send him, oh send him,
Oh send our old sergeant to hell, to hell.
Oh keep him, oh keep him,
Oh keep the old bastard in hell.

I once took my girl for a ramble,
Along a nice old shady lane.
She caught her right foot in a bramble,
And arse over titties she came.

REPEAT CHORUS.

Oh! Sergeant, oh, sergeant,
Don't pinch my rum ration from me,
From me. Oh sergeant, oh sergeant,
Bring back my rum ration to me.

REPEAT CHORUS.

'The Soldier's Prayer'

Probably sung to a traditional folk-song tune, it was sometimes spoken as a monologue.

A soldier and a sailor were talking one day.
Said the soldier to the sailor, 'Let us both kneel and pray.
And for each thing that we pray for, may we also have ten,
At the end of each chorus we will both say Amen!'

'What shall we pray for? We'll pray for some beer,
Glorious, glorious, glorious beer!
And if we have one pint may we also have ten.
May we have a fucking brewery,' said the sailor. 'Amen!'

'The next thing we'll pray for, we'll pray for some love.
We hope he will send it to us from above.
And if we get one girl may we also have ten.
May we get a knocking shop,' said the soldier. 'Amen.'

'The next thing we'll pray for, we'll pray for our Queen.
What a kind hearted bastard to us she has been,
And if she has one son may she also have ten.
May she get a football team,' said the sailor. 'Amen.'

The next thing we'll pray for we'll pray for some leave,
Glorious, wonderful, marvellous leave.
And if we get one day may we also get ten,
May we get a month of Sundays,' they both said. 'Amen.'

'Now all you young officers and NCOs too,
With your hands at your sides and with fuck all to do,

When you stand on parade abusing us men,
May the Lord come and fuck all of you,' they both said.'Amen.'

'They Were Only Playing Leap Frog'

Tune: 'John Brown's Body'

This reflected the much-believed fact that staff officers did nothing but amuse themselves all day and the ludicrous thought of them playing leapfrog amused most Tommies.

One grass-hopper jumped right over
Another grass-hopper's back,
And another grass-hopper jumped right over
That other grass-hopper's back.
A third grass hopper jumped right over
The two grass-hoppers' backs,
And a fourth grass-hopper jumped right over
All the other grass-hoppers' backs.

CHORUS:
They were only playing leap frog,
They were only playing leap frog,
They were only playing leap frog,
When one grass-hopper jumped right over
Another grass-hopper's back.

One staff officer jumped right over
Another staff officer's back,
And another staff officer jumped right over
That other staff officer's back.

A third staff officer jumped right over
The two staff officers' backs,
And a fourth staff officer jumped right over
All the other staff officers' backs.

REPEAT CHORUS.

(One of the many other variations is as follows)
We were only drawing water,
We were only drawing water,
We were only drawing water,
When the sergeant major came and stole
The handle off the pump.

Glory, glory, how peculiar!
Glory, glory, how peculiar!
Glory, glory, how peculiar!
He stole the handle off the pump!

'This Is The Flying Corps'

Tune: 'There Is A Happy Land'

The 'four' is a reference to the pre-war four-year period of enlistment.

This is the Flying Corps,
So people say,
Where air mechanics
Lay the drains,
For two bob a day.

Oh! You should hear them sing,
'Roll on when my four is in,
Then back home my hook I'll sling,
And there I'll stay.'

'Tickler's Jam'

Still more words on the subject of jam, this time dating from its issue during the Gallipoli campaign of 1915.

Tickler's jam. Tickler's jam.
How we love old Tickler's jam.
Packed in Blighty in one-pound pots,
Sent from England in ten-ton lots.
Every night when I'm asleep,
I'm dreaming that I'm
Forcing my way through the Dardanelles,
With Tommy Tickler's jam.

'Tiddlewinks Old Man'

Tune: 'Sailors' Hornpipe'

Another nonsense song usually sung by officers, in the same vein as 'Do Your Balls Hang Low?'

Tiddlewinks, old man,
Find a woman if you can,
If you can't find a woman,
Do without old man.

When the rock of Gibraltar
Takes a flying leap at Malta,
You'll never get your bullocks in a corned beef can.

'Wash Me In The Water'

Based on a Salvation Army hymn. Its military use is believed to pre-date the First World War, although its origin is now lost.

Wash Me In The water
We Are But Private Soldiers
We Beat 'Em
We Haven't Seen The Sergeant
We're Here Because We're Here
We've Had No Beer

What A Rotten Song
What Did You Join The Army For?
When The Stew Is On The Table
When This Lousy War Is Over
When Very Lights Are Shining
Where Are Our Uniforms?
Who Killed Cock Robin?

'We Are But Private Soldiers'

Tune: 'We Are But Little Children Weak'

We are but private soldiers weak,
Our pay is only seven bob a week.
What e'er we do by night or day,
It makes no difference to our pay.
Our hours a day are twenty four,
And thank the Lord there are no more.
For if there were we know that we
Would work another two or three.
There is one thing we do believe,
That we're entitled to some leave.
We don't know why we're so cursed,
We'll get our old age pension first.

'We Beat 'Em'

Tune: 'Coming Through The Rye'

Dating from around the time of the battle of Loos (September 1915) it reflected some early signs of war weariness creeping in. Post-1916 this became much more pronounced in songs and chants.

We beat 'em on the Marne,
We beat 'em on the Aisne,
They gave us hell at Neuve-Chapelle,
But here we go again.

'We Haven't Seen The Sergeant'

Tune: 'He's A Cousin Of Mine'

This song was personalized depending on what regiment and platoon were singing it.

> We haven't seen the sergeant for a hell of a time,
> A hell of a time, a hell of a time.
> A came up to see what we were doin',
> Number Four Platoon will be his ruin.
> Oh we haven't seen the sergeant for a hell of a time,
> Perhaps he's gone up with a mine.
> He's a sergeant in the Rifle Brigade,
> Well, strafe him, he's no cousin of mine.

'We're Here Because We're Here'

Tune: 'Auld Lang Syne'

A song much beloved by the soldiers, as most of the time they really had little idea of where they were going, or what they were supposed to be doing when they got there.

> We're here
> Because we're here,
> Because we're here,
> Because we're here.
>
> We're here
> Because we're here,

Because we're here,
Because we're here.

'We've Had No Beer'

Tune: 'Lead, Kindly Light'

The ever-popular complaint of the soldier, insufficient beer.

We've had no beer,
We've had no beer to-day.
We've had no beer,
We've had no beer,
No beer at all today.
We've had no beer,
We've had no beer today.

'What A Rotten Song'

Oh my! What a rotten song,
What a rotten song,
What a rotten song,
Oh my! What a rotten song,
And what a rotten singer too.

'What Did You Join The Army For?'

Tune: 'Here's To The Maiden Of Bashful Fifteen'

This tune was the regimental march of the King's Liverpool Regiment and was adopted pre-war.

> What did you join the army for?
> What did you join the army for?
> What did you join the army for?
> You must have been bloody well barmy.

'When The Stew Is On The table'

Tune: 'When The Roll Is Called Up Yonder'

> When the stew is on the table,
> When the stew is on the table,
> When the stew is on the table,
> When the stew is on the table, I'll be there.

> When the beer is in the tankard,
> When the beer is in the tankard,
> When the beer is in the tankard,
> When the beer is in the tankard, I'll be there.

'When This Lousy War Is Over'

Tune: Hymn, 'What A Friend We Have In Jesus'

When this lousy war is over,
No more soldiering for me.
When I get my civvie clothes on,
Oh, how happy I shall be.
No more church parades on Sunday,
No more asking for a pass.
I shall tell the sergeant major
To stick his passes up his arse.

When this lousy war is over,
Oh, how happy I shall be.
When I get my civvie clothes on,
And I return from Germany.
I shall sound my own reveille,
I shall make my own tattoo.
No more NCOs to bollock me,
No more rotten army stew.

NCOs will all be navvies,
Privates ride in motor cars.
Officers will smoke their Woodbines,
Privates puff their big cigars.
No more 'Stand-To' in the trenches,
Never another church parade,
No more shiv'ring on the fire step,
No more Tickler's marmalade.

The Pess-Optimist. "Wot a life! No rest, no beer, no nuffin. It's only us keeping so
cheerful as pulls us through!" (Punch)

'When Very Lights Are Shining'

Tune: 'When Irish Eyes Are Smiling'

When Very lights are shining,
Sure they're like the morning light.
And when the guns begin to thunder,
You can hear the angel's shite.
Then the Maxims start to chatter,
And trench mortars send a few,
And when Very lights are shining,
'Tis time for a rum issue.

When Very lights are shining,
Sure 'tis like the morning dew.
And when shells begin a-bursting,
It makes you think your time's come too.
And when you start advancing,
Five nines and gas comes through,
Sure when Very lights are shining,
'Tis rum or lead for you.

'Where Are Our Uniforms?'

Tune: 'There Is a Happy Land, Far, Far, Away'

This short chant can be dated to 1914, when everything
– uniforms, rifles, food – was in short supply for the huge
numbers of men who had flocked to join the army.

Where are our uniforms?
Far, far, away.
When will our rifles come?
P'raps, p'raps some day.
All we need is just a gun,
For to chase the bloody Hun.
Think of us when we are gone,
Far, far away.

'Who Killed Cock Robin?'

Primarily an RFC/RAF monologue. Based on the pre-war rhyme 'Cock Robin'.

Who Killed Cock Robin?

'I,' said the Hun,

'With my machine gun,

I killed Cock Robin.'

CHORUS:

All the pilots who were there

Said, 'Fuck it, we will chuck it,'

When they heard Cock Robin,

had kicked the fucking bucket.

When they heard Cock Robin

Had kicked the bucket.

Who saw him hit?

'I' said old Fritz,

'I saw him hit,

And I saw him fall in bits.'

REPEAT CHORUS.

Who saw him die?

'I' said the spy,

'With my beady eye

I saw him die.'

REPEAT CHORUS.

Then all the pilots in the air
Went a strafing and a bombin',
When they heard of the death
Of poor Cock Robin.

'Yes, And We Can Do It'

Tune: Nursery song, 'In And Out Of The Window'

A story in six verses, aimed at the niggling discipline in the army, in this instance the heinous crime of parading with a button undone.

Breaking out of barracks.
Breaking out of barracks.
Breaking out of barracks.
As you have done before.
Parading all unbuttoned,
Parading all unbuttoned.
Parading all unbuttoned.
As you have done before.

Take his name and number.
Take his name and number.
Take his name and number.
As you have done before.

Up before the CO,
Up before the CO,
Up before the CO,
As you have done before.

Fourteen days detention,
Fourteen days detention,
Fourteen days detention,
As you have done before.

Pack-drill, bread and water,
Pack-drill, bread and water,
Pack-drill, bread and water,
As you have done before.

Yes, and we can do it,
Yes, and we can do it,
Yes, and we can do it,
As we have done before.

APPENDICES

Appendix 1 – The Signaller's Phonetic Alphabet

	Regular army, 1914	**Army of 1918**
A	Ack	Apples
B	Beer	Butter
C	Cork	Charlie
D	Don	Duff
E	Eddy	Edward
F	Freddy	Freddie
G	George	George
H	Harry	Harry
I	Ink	Ink
J	Jug	Johnnie
K	King	King
L	London	London
M	Emma	Monkey
N	Nuts	Nuts
O	Orange	Orange
P	Pip	Pudding
Q	Quad	Queenie
R	Robert	Robert
S	Esses	Sugar
T	Toc	Tommy
U	Uncle	Uncle
V	Vic	Vic
W	William	William
X	Xerxes	X-ray
Y	Yellow	Yorker
Z	Zebra	Zebra

Appendix 2 – British Military Units

Formation	Commander	Approximate Manpower	Notes
Army	General or Field Marshal	85,000	2 corps plus HQ staff and attached army troops (signallers, mortars, machine gunners etc) made up an army.
Army Corps	Lieutenant General	38,500	2 divisions plus HQ staff and attached corps troops made up a corps.
Division	Major General	18,000	3 brigades plus HQ staff and divisional troops made up a division.
Brigade	Brigadier General	4,000	4 battalions plus HQ staff made up a brigade.
Battalion	Lieutenant Colonel	1,000	4 companies plus HQ staff made up a battalion.
Company	Major or Captain	220	4 platoons plus HQ staff made up a company.
Platoon	Lieutenant or 2nd lieutenant	52	Four sections made up a platoon.
Section	NCO	13	

Appendix 3 – The Hymn of Hate

French and Russian they matter not,
A blow for a blow and a shot for a shot;
We love them not, we hate them not,
We hold the Weichsel and Vosges-gate.
We have but one and only hate,
We love as one, we hate as one,
We have one foe and one alone.
He is known to you all, he is known to you all,
He crouches behind the dark grey flood,
Full of envy, of rage, of craft, of gall,
Cut off by waves that are thicker than blood.
Come, let us stand at the Judgement place,
An oath to swear to, face to face,
An oath of bronze no wind can shake,
An oath for our sons and their sons to take.
Come, hear the word, repeat the word,
Throughout the Fatherland make it heard.
We will never forego our hate.
We have but one single hate,
We love as one, we hate as one,
We have one foe, and one alone –
ENGLAND!

Take you the folk of the Earth in pay,
With bars of gold your ramparts lay.
Bedeck the ocean with bow on bow,
Ye reckon well, but not well enough now.
French and Russian, they matter not,
A blow for a blow, a shot for a shot,
We fight the battle with bronze and steel,

And the time that is coming Peace will seal.
You we will hate with a lasting hate,
We will never forego our hate.
Hate by water and hate by land,
Hate of the head and hate of the hand,
Hate of the hammer and hate of the crown,
Hate of seventy millions choking down.
We love as one, we hate as one,
We have one foe and one alone –
ENGLAND!

Appendix 4 – Tommy Atkins

The first printed use of 'Tommy Atkins' was in a poem written in 1899 by Private A. Smith of the Black Watch to commemorate their part in the battle of Magersfontein during the Second Boer War.

> Such was the day for our regiment,
> Dread the revenge we will take.
> Dearly we paid for the blunder,
> A drawing-room general's mistake.
> Why weren't we told of the trenches?
> Why weren't we told of the wire?
> Why were we marched up in column,
> May Tommy Atkins enquire ...

Appendix 5 – Inscription on the Headstone of the Unknown Warrior, Westminster Abbey

'Beneath this stone rests the body of a British warrior unknown by name or rank, brought from France to lie among the most illustrious of the land and buried here on Armistice Day, in November 1920, in the presence of His Majesty King George V, his Ministers of State, and the Chiefs of his Forces, and a vast concourse of the nation. Thus are commemorated the many multitudes who during the Great War of 1914–18 gave the most that man can give, life itself, for God, for King and country, for loved ones, home and Empire, for the sacred cause of justice and the freedom of the world. They buried him among the Kings because he had done good toward God and toward his house.'

Appendix 6 – Honours and Awards

This covers only the period of the Great War. The requirements for awards for many medals changed greatly in the post-war years.

VC Victoria Cross. Introduced by Queen Victoria on 29 January 1856, and manufactured from bronze cannon captured during the Crimean War, it was the highest British award for 'valour in the face of the enemy'. Any serving soldier, seaman or airforce personnel from Britain of the Commonwealth was eligible. 628 were awarded in the First World War.

DSO Distinguished Service Order. Introduced in 1888 for meritorious or distinguished service, it was usually, but not exclusively, awarded to officers of the rank of captain or above.

DSC Distinguished Service Cross. It was originally instigated in 1901 as the Conspicuous Service Cross, for award to naval warrant and junior officers who did not qualify for the DSO. It was renamed the Distinguished Service Cross in October 1914, and the award was extended to all naval officers below the rank of lieutenant commander.

MC Military Cross. The award was created in 1914 for all commissioned officers under the rank of captain and for warrant officers for acts of bravery in the field.

DFC Distinguished Flying Cross. Introduced in June 1918, for all RAF commissioned officers and warrant officers for 'An act or acts of valour, courage or devotion to duty whilst flying in active operations against the enemy'.

AFC Air Force Cross. Introduced in June 1918, for commissioned officers and warrant officers for 'An act or acts of valour, courage or devotion to duty whilst flying, though not in active operations against the enemy'.

DCM Distinguished Conduct Medal. Introduced in 1854, it was a relatively high-level award for any non-commissioned officer or other ranks for acts of courage whilst on active service.

CGM Conspicuous Gallantry Medal. Established in July 1874, it was awarded to commissioned ranks or below, for conspicuous gallantry in action against the enemy at sea or, latterly, in the air.

DSM Distinguished Service Medal. Introduced in October 1914, it could be awarded to any naval rank up to and including the rank of chief petty officer for bravery or resourcefulness on active service at sea.

MM Military Medal. Established in March 1916, it was the other ranks' equivalent to the Military Cross. Warrant officers could be awarded either the MC or the MM.

DFM Distinguished Flying Medal. Established in June 1918, it was the other ranks' equivalent to the Distinguished Flying Cross. It could also be awarded to commissioned officers and warrant officers, who were also eligible for the DFC.

AFM Air Force Medal. Introduced in June 1918 as the other ranks' equivalent of the Air Force Cross. As with most other RAF awards, warrant officers were also eligible for it.

MSM Meritorious Service Medal. Instituted in December 1845 for the British Army, it recognized meritorious service by non-commissioned officers. Unusually, recipients were granted an annuity, the amount of which was based on rank. Between 1916 and 1919, army NCOs could be awarded the medal immediately for meritorious service in the field but they could also be awarded the medal for acts of non-combat gallantry.

MiD Mentioned in Dispatches. This was not a medal, but was recognition of a soldier's gallant or meritorious action in the face of the enemy. The soldier's name appeared in an official report written by a superior officer and sent to the high command. The award was indicated by a small brass oak leaf, worn on the medal ribbon of the 1914–18 Victory Medal.

Appendix 7 – Sniper Sandy

Sandy Mac the sniper is a-sniping from his loophole,
With a telescopic rifle he is looking for the Hun.
If he sees a sniper lurking or a working party working,
At once he opens fire on them every one.
And when you come into our trench, by night-time or by day,
We take you to his loophole, and we point to him and say:

CHORUS:
Sniper Sandy's slaying Saxon soldiers,
And Saxon soldiers seldom show but Sandy has a few.
And every day the Bosches put up little wooden crosses,
In the cemetery for Saxon soldiers sniper Sandy slew.

Now in the German trenches there's a sniper they call Hermann,
A stout and solid Saxon with a healthy growth of beard.
And Hermann with his rifle is pride of every German,
Until our Sandy gets on to him, and Hermann gets afeared.
For when he hears the bullets come he slides down to the ground,
And trembling he gasps out to his comrades all around:

REPEAT CHORUS.

The Seaforths got so proud of Sandy's prowess with his rifle,
They drew up a report on him and sent it to the Corps.
And ninety-seven was his bag – it doesn't seem a trifle,
But Sandy isn't certain that it wasn't even more.
And when Sir Douglas heard of it he broke into a laugh,
And rubbed his hands and chuckled to the Chief of General Staff:

REPEAT CHORUS.

Appendix 8 – Translation of 'Adieu La Vie (Chanson De Craonne)'

When at the end of a week's leave, we're going to go back to the trenches. Our place there is so useful that without us they'd take a thrashing. But it's all over now, we've had it up to here, nobody wants to march anymore and with hearts downcast, like when you're sobbing, we're saying good-bye to the civilians. Even if we don't get drums, even if we don't get trumpets we're leaving for up there with lowered heads.

Chorus:

Good-bye to life, good-bye to love, good-bye to all the women. It's all over now, we've had it for good with this awful war. It's at Craonne up on the plateau that we're leaving our skins, 'cause we've all been sentenced to die. We're the ones that they're sacrificing.

Repeat chorus.

Eight days in the trenches, eight days of suffering, and yet we still have hope that tonight the relief will come that we keep waiting for. Suddenly in the silent night we hear someone approach. It's an infantry officer who's coming to take over from us. Quietly in the shadows under a falling rain the poor soldiers are going to look at their graves.

Repeat chorus.

On the grand boulevards it's hard to look at all the rich and powerful whooping it up. For them life is good but for us it's not the same. Instead of hiding, all these shirkers would do better to go up to the trenches to defend what they have, because we have nothing. All of us poor wretches, all our comrades are being buried there to defend the wealth of these gentlemen here.

REPEAT CHORUS.

Those who have the dough, they'll be coming back, 'cause it's for them that we're dying. But it's all over now, 'cause all of the footsloggers are going to go on strike. It'll be your turn, all you rich and powerful gentlemen, to go up onto the plateau. And if you want to make war, then pay for it with your own skins.

SELECT BIBLIOGRAPHY

Baker, R.A., *British Music Hall, An Illustrated History* (Sutton, Stroud, 2005).

Brophy, J., *Songs and Slang of the British Soldier* (Scholartis Press, London, 1931).

Brophy J. and E. Partridge, *The Long Trail* (Sphere, London, 1969).

Grose, F., *A Classical Dictionary of the Vulgar Tongue* (Amberley, London 1971).

Oxford English Dictionary (Oxford University Press, New York, 1979).

Partridge, E., *A Dictionary of Slang and Unconventional English* (Butler and Tanner, London, 1937).

Rust, B. ed., *Gramophone Records of the First World War* (David and Charles, Newton Abbot, 1991).

The Wipers Times (reprint by Little Books, London, 2006).

ABOUT THE AUTHOR

In the 1980s Martin Pegler had the privilege of interviewing many
First World War veterans about their wartime experiences, and the
recordings are now part of the sound archives of the Imperial War
Museum, London, as well as being the inspiration behind this
collection.

Martin now lives in the Somme, France, where he and his wife run a
bed and breakfast business, situated on top of the old German front
line at Combles, from where he also runs motorcycle tours of the
battlefields. He is the author of a number of books on military history
and acts as a firearms consultant for various film and television
companies. Since 2011 he has been one of the militaria specialists on
the Antiques Roadshow.